JAPAN COUNTRY LIVING

SPIRIT ⋆ TRADITION ⋆ STYLE

AMY SYLVESTER KATOH
PRINCIPAL PHOTOGRAPHY BY SHIN KIMURA

TUTTLE PUBLISHING
Boston • Rutland, Vermont • Tokyo

ACKNOWLEDGEMENTS

For my family: to Yuichi, who first started me on this journey, to Mia and Saya, Tai and Toshi, who are always beside me. And for Toshiko and Sueko, who light the way. This book would have been impossible without the kindness and cooperation of countless people. Heartfelt thanks to the Akagi family, Mr. and Mrs. Akiyama, J.C. Brown, Diane Durston, Koji Fujibayashi of Sanso Murata, Kozo Fujita, Hiroko Izumi Fukuchi, Mr. and Mrs. Hagiwara, Mr. and Mrs. Hagiya, the Hiroji Hashimoto family, the Junji Hata family, Dr. Hide Ishiguro, Senzo Ishikawa, Koji Kado, Kame no Ii, Yoshihiro Kamitani, the Hiromi Kanemaru family, the Kawasaki family, Yufuin, Kyushu, Marc Keane, Miwako Kimura, Ryoichi Kinoshita, Nanyen Kitamuro, Yuri Konomi, Hiroshi Kurata, Hitoshi Kutsukake, Mr. and Mrs. Richard Large, Kiyoko Machida, Mitsu Minowa, Akio Mitsuno, Daisuke Miyashita, Mr. and Mrs. Miyatani, Sachi Mohri, Mr. and Mrs. Mori, Mr. and Mrs. Tadashi Morita, the Murata family, Makoto Nakano, Takashi Nakazato, the Nibe family, Takako Nishikawa, Margaret Price, Shinji Sakamoto and mother, Shinsaburo Shibuya, Nobuyoshi Shimomura, Mr. and Mrs. Hiroyuki Shindo, Masanosuke Shirawaka, Barbara Stephan, Shinji Takagi, Yoichi Takimoto, Kenji Tsuchisawa, Mr. and Mrs. Uchida, Mr. and Mrs. Masao Umesao, Douglas and Kiyo Woodruff, Akemitsu Yamada, Mr. and Mrs. Yanagida, and Kazuko Yoshiura.

Endpapers, Whipped green tea and a citron on a table of old boat timber, Yu Craft Gallery, Kanazawa. Pages 2-3, A rare sight today, a solitary thatched farmhouse, Miyama-cho, Kyoto Prefecture. Pages 4-5, Cotton indigo tie-dyed (*shibori*) crepe work jacket in a field of newly harvested rice. Pages 6-7, Circular rice field dedicated to the gods of the grain; outdoor folk museum, Takayama, Gifu Prefecture. Pages 10-11, Persimmons drying against an old house, Noto Peninsula.

Photos pp. 50-51 & 54 © Akira Kita   Photos pp. 14-15, 38-39, 145 © Naoki Baba.

Published by Tuttle Publishing, an imprint of Periplus Editions (HK) Ltd.

LCC Card No. 93-60522
ISBN 0-8048-1858-4

First published, 1993
Printed in Singapore

Designed by Katharine Markulin Hama

Distributed by:

North America, Latin America & Europe
Tuttle Publishing
364 Innovation Drive, North Clarendon, VT 05759-9436.
Tel: (802) 773 8930; Fax: (802) 773 6993 Email: info@tuttlepublishing.com
www.tuttlepublishing.com

Japan
Tuttle Publishing
Yaekari Building, 3rd Floor, 5-4-12 Osaki, Shinagawa-ku, Tokyo 141-0032
Tel: (03) 5437 0171; Fax: (03) 5437 0755 Email: tuttle-sales@gol.com

Asia Pacific
Berkeley Books Pte Ltd
130 Joo Seng Road, #06-01, Singapore 368357
Tel: (65) 6280 1330; Fax: (65) 6280 6290 Email: inquiries@periplus.com.sg
www. periplus.com

05 07 09 10 08 06
2 4 6 8 7 5 3

CONTENTS

◆

THE ROAD THROUGH THE COUNTRY

On first impression, Japan was a jumble of colors, shapes, sounds, smells and people. Patches of brilliant green rice fields bordered by sluices of

running water, layers of indigo mountains, explosions of scarlet spider lilies at the edges of the fields, and people in blue-and-white work clothes, planting, pruning, picking. Here and there a wooden shrine or a stone statue, graced perhaps with a red bib and a fresh offering of flowers, a rope of twisted straw, several coins. Farmhouse roofs were thatched—thick bonnets of golden reeds that turned brown, then gray. Sculpted, organic toppings, the roofs looked as though they had been poured over the house.

In the myths, the islands of Japan are said to have been created of drops falling from the spear of the founding god as it was drawn from the ocean. Standing on the hills, overlooking the misty folds of the land, the myth becomes real and I think that, yes, this must have been how Japan began.

Mostly the gods created mountains. There are flat places and plains, but it is the the mountains that circumscribed and prevented man from seeing or understanding what was beyond—and also bonding people together and unifying them in common experience. In the mountains reside the spirits, the anima, that invest the earth and are objects of awe.

Today the road through the countryside of Japan is

cluttered with telephone poles and wires, an avalanche of signs, posters, plastic flowers, and rusting cars, the neon flash of love hotels and the ubiquitous pachinko parlors. Everywhere there is clutter, visual chaos, the blight of consumerism on the land.

The land is a natural beauty. And the road we seek is a dream—a road that meanders through mountains and country villages of thatched houses, where people still wear indigo work clothes in the fields, with bamboo baskets beside them. The fruits of their fields are on the table in pots from nearby kilns, paper-covered lanterns light the room as they sit around an open hearth mending clothes or weaving straw sandals.

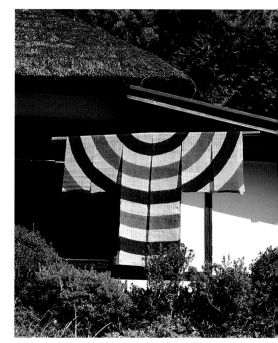

Traditional country life was never easy, nor was it the rustic ideal that twentieth-century romantics try to conjure up in reply to the mechanized plastic dream world that has captured favor today. Ironically, the very prosperity that everyone welcomes is destroying the country values of resourcefulness and ingenuity and creativity, which evolved from a life of subsistence without surfeit. Until very recently in this country, life was harsh and survival difficult. The ability to make do with little and stretch possibilities to their limits allowed Japanese farmer and fisherman to endure and are the backbone of Japan's present affluence. Yet, such values seem to have no place or function in the

affluent and powerful Japan of today. Something important has been lost. While poverty is hardly desirable, there should be some means of keeping alive the wisdom it engendered.

The ingenuity, vigor, and creativity of rural Japan of the past may still be found. We can dip our buckets into the waters of time, when people were forced to make what they needed to live with, to eat with, to pray and play with. By going to the countryside, by relating to and living with things made by country craftsmen, farmers, fishermen and their wives, one can touch the values that imbued Japan with vitality. Country things were made to be used. Their beauty comes from that utility and earns our admiration just because it is not trying to attract attention or be beautiful. The unassuming nature of country things is what appeals to me.

Before the old could vanish entirely, I put together this book, searching for the road least traveled, taking old paths and new, real and ideal, to create a collage that will give a taste of country Japan. Sometimes essences of the country are found in the city, or in the tiny spaces of public housing developments. Sometimes they exist in the mind. Flashes of country spirit—the unselfconscious genius of country Japan past and present, in houses, food, craft, work, and play—can be found in unexpected places. I have chosen a mixture of traditional and contemporary as well here to represent the honesty, the strength, the charm, the beauty, and the quirkiness of country Japan. Join me on this trip through a Japan little

seen and little appreciated. The journey can give meaning, humor, and beauty to our own lives. It is a road once taken never forgotten, a journey that for me will never end. ◼

COUNTRY HOUSES

Japanese folk houses have their origins in the tropical climate of Southeast Asia, and they have changed remarkably little despite the inhospitable climate of Japan. This architecture is effective during Japan's humid summers; it makes little provision for keeping warm in winter, or for privacy. The post and beam construction provides shelter against rains, earthquakes and typhoons. It can accommodate movable walls and thick roofs of thatch and can take the weight of heavy snow. A veranda (*engawa*) under the wide overhang of the roof provides a natural transition between the rooms within and nature without.

Houses were made of what the land offered, largely wood and straw, earth, bamboo, and paper. Roofs were always covered in the materials available in that area—thatch, shingles, grasses, bark, even stone in certain regions. Floors and walls were usually constructed of earth. In houses in northern Japan, it was not uncommon to find the family animals sheltered along with the rest of the household.

Walking into a Japanese farmhouse, the immediate reaction is visceral rather than cerebral. First impressions are of dark, of clutter, of jumble. Here is something of the earth, organic, alive, an extension of the land. The smells, the sights, the sounds are a meeting point between man and his environment. The Japanese farmhouse does not exclude nature, it is not a fortress. It is part of nature, and embraces it at every juncture.

The beauty of the traditional Japanese house was in the sensitive use of natural materials. Such a house was filled with ingenious ways in which man gave shape to his living environment. Poverty acted as a creative force to strengthen ingenuity and deftness. There was an overall harmony between man, his environment, and his way of living. Piety and respect for materials were evident throughout. Bamboo, wood, earth, paper, and straw were used in the most basic ways to keep the house standing and

hold it together, both literally and figuratively. Proportions were easy and natural, based on a human scale. Ceilings were generally high, giving a feeling of space even in smaller rooms. And, too, the ceilings were textural and organic, often made of bound bamboo or of bare boards.

Upper floors were used as work or storage areas, sometimes reserved for silkworm cultivation. Windows were few. Generally it was sliding doors and screens that opened to give light and air and access to the outside. Though the floor plans of farmhouses have many regional variations, individual room arrangement was vague and unspecific. Each room was simple, basic, and nonpersonal; anyone could use a room for nearly any purpose. Private space was not provided or even a consideration.

At the heart of the farmhouse was the fire. Generally this was in an open hearth (*irori*), a stone- or clay-lined pit sunk beneath the floor and filled with fine ash, in the middle of which charcoal was constantly kept burning. Over this a long decorative pot-hook (*jizai-kagi*) was suspended from a beam, and at the end hung a cast-iron pot or tea kettle.

Fire was an important presence in the house. Somewhere, in the irori or in a hibachi, it was kept burning at all times to keep a kettle boiling, things over the fire drying, food cooking. There was always the smell of the fire and of smoke. Smoke pervaded every crevice of the house. Smoke kept taut the straw ropes used to tie together beams, rafters,

and thatch. People gathered around the hearth for warmth and to cook food, while overhead the smoke worked to dry foods, implements, and clothes. The irori was the gathering place for all members of the family. Old people rarely left it; their job was to tend the fire and the grandchildren while others worked.

The household altars—both Buddhist and Shinto—were, and still are, an omnipresent feature of the Japanese farmhouse. The gods and ancestors looked over the well-being of the household from their high place and protected the family. They were prayed to daily. The first food of the meal would be served to the gods before the family ate. The house, with its gods and fires, its natural materials, was a living presence, connecting man with his natural surroundings.

Kitchens were cold, dark, and usually only vaguely differentiated, sometimes little more than a corner of the dirt-floored indoor work area (*doma*). Running water and plumbing are both recent luxuries, as is gas for cooking. The bath and toilet were usually separate and outside, although recently, they have been included in the main house. Flush toilets even today are far from universal, and gradually, wood-fired baths have disappeared.

These once typical Japanese farmhouses have nearly vanished now. Simple and human proportions, natural materials masterfully utilized, inside-outside continuity, connectedness—the pillar of the genius of Japanese architecture is surely the honest farmhouse.

(to page 29)

If one searches, scenes reminiscent of Japan's past still appear. People live simply, in tune with the rhythms of the land.

Only rarely, deep in the countryside, do you find clusters of thatched farmhouses. When I do, my heart leaps. I almost feel them before I see them, and when I look up, I see a friend. Even if no one is living in them, those straw and earth walls are alive. They are unspeakably beautiful and uncannily human, being of the same organic matter that we are. What will be the legacy of the plastic replacements that now plague the land? What will a child think of his or her heritage, never having seen the eloquent predecessors?

But, you never know. Once I was driving with friends through the mountains northwest of Kyoto in the late summer. The rice was a brilliant green. Layers of mountains surrounded us, mostly hidden in the mists. As we turned yet another curve in the road, suddenly a perfect, newly thatched house appeared, surrounded by rice fields and their guardian scarecrows with the misty mountains behind. Before the house a grandmother held a baby in her arms. We had to stop. When we asked why they decided to thatch their farmhouse, the grandmother smiled and replied that the young people, her son-in-law and daughter, wanted it. It cost more, she said proudly, but it was worth it. ◨

Inside-Outside

All the exterior and interior sliding doors and screens of a traditional Japanese house can be pushed aside or removed to open the entire structure to the outside and allow wind, sunlight, and even birds to penetrate to the heart of the house. The separation between inside and outside vanishes for the

moment, and the entire house becomes a part of the natural surroundings, defined only by the roof and the raised, tatami-matted floor. This appealing feature is hardly possible with the traditional Western house, which is more like a fortress against the outside and a rebuttal of the elements. Whatever the cultural and historical reasons, this simplicity and flexibility of interior space and the careful blurring of distinctions between interior and exterior have fascinated and inspired the world's architects for the past century.

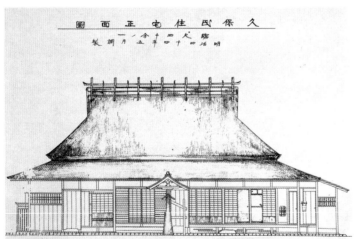

Top: Snow dusts the roof of the Shindo house in winter.
Above left: The plan of the Woodruff house exterior.
Above right: The entranceway to the Shindo house is welcoming, even on a cold gray day.

Opposite page, top: Woodblocks of houses and shops decorate an old ticket.
Below: A man and his dog in the snowy landscape of a hamlet of thatched houses in Miyama-cho, Kyoto Prefecture.

Following page: Gates were sometimes elaborate in country houses. Imposing doors, sometimes topped with a tiled gable, gave stature and importance to the household.

LIVING IN THE COUNTRY

Over the years I have been invited into and have had the chance to see the interiors of those wonderful Japanese thatched houses, which have so much appeal viewed from the roadside, tucked up against mountains at the edge of a valley's rice fields. Such houses have a life and character of their own. They speak to you immediately upon entering.

One unforgettable house was on a road in the middle of the Noto Peninsula. My friends and I caught sight of a noble roof soaring above the road. We walked up the hill and found that the house was even more impressive than it had seemed from below. The architecture commanded our attention, a rare and precious token of the past. The lady of the house was just stepping out of the barn, a purple crocheted sweater over her apron, and when we asked if we could look around, she smiled with a mixture of embarrassment and surprise, saying that it was old and dirty and we wouldn't be interested. But secretly she seemed pleased at our interest in her family compound, where she had lived all her married life. She quickly darted inside and alerted her husband, who, when he appeared, was frailer and older than she and had simply put a thick jacket over his pajamas to greet us. Both happily showed us their house and outbuildings and told us some of its history. The main structure was built 350 years ago, a massive fortress against snow and cold, which once was considerable. Some parts had been added, other parts restored. Up until forty years ago, the roof was thatched, but when that proved to be too much to keep up, they converted to a tile roof. The open courtyard from where we viewed the house was fronted by the main building, clearly the living quarters. Persimmons drying on cords festooned one wall. Small, hot red peppers were drying, too, and onions from the garden. Tools of the years and ladders were hung against the storehouse.

The elderly couple was somewhat taken aback by our unbridled rapture for their house. They had some ambivalence as to the value of preserving old houses. To some extent, it implies that one does not have enough money to rebuild something new and modern and convenient. Old and dirty are synonymous, and anyone who still lives in an old house is considered dirty and probably poor. Family reputation is involved. These two will continue to keep this house going as long as they can, but they are old. What will happen when they die? Who will carry on? Will the next generation be content to live in this relatively inconvenient way?

We, outsiders who have come from cities and from other countries, gasp at this massive and handsome piece of Japan's country heritage, and urge its owners to preserve and treasure the house and the lifestyle as they have the persimmons so painstakingly hung from the rafters.

Another thrilling moment was on a trip through Miyama-cho, one of the remotest parts of Kyoto Prefecture, during the preparation of this book. We were honored by an unusual sight—a group of thatchers repairing the roof of a farmhouse. Like a woman lifting her skirts, the cover of the house had been raised and removed, and the supporting rafters were visible, spread at the base and tied together at the top. Smoky bamboo poles

were being lashed on horizontally across the rafters, and thatch was being attached to them, stitched with a fat wooden needle and twisted straw twine. The beams and rafters were tied together with bindings of rice-straw rope. The village was made up of thatched houses, their distinctive straw bonnets dotting the land. I was amazed again at how utterly basic it all is—the structures, the materials, the landscape—and how incomparably beautiful.

In a changing world, traditional values break down and are replaced by new values of comfort, privacy, and consumerism. Country farms no longer support extended farm families, so men seek work in the cities and leave

traditional country villages empty. Sons and daughters follow. Houses lie vacant and soon start to return to the earth from which they came, or are quickly dispatched with chainsaw and bulldozer and carted off to a local dump. I find myself searching in quiet desperation for these old friends, which seem to have been there until very recently. Gradually they fall into disuse, and a new plastic replacement is built. This is thought to be beautiful because it is clean (which is the same word as beautiful in the Japanese language). Clean it may be, but not satisfying, and its "beauty" will fade quickly, since it lacks the inner beauty and honesty of structure and material of its predecessors.

The question of heritage remains. What is it? How do we treat it? How does it fit in our lives? The easiest way is to tear old things down and replace them with the fashion of the moment. Clean, quick and cheap. In Japan, prefabricated houses replace structures built to last for centuries. But the hasty solution is empty and doesn't touch the soul. It leaves a vacuum, spiritual and aesthetic, that traditional country houses used to fill, and interrupts the rhythm of life, which traditional houses used to engender.

Country Kaleidoscope

The rhythms of the agricultural year set the pace of country life, and these rhythms still center around rice. This cycle of life, which was so fundamental to Japan until quite recently, is hardly felt in the cities. In tiny fields, clever machines now plant and harvest rice, though older people often hold out and do this work by hand. Similarly, rice is now usually dried mechanically, in hot air blowers, but often a farmer will sun-dry some of his harvest, mainly for his own family. Sun-drying is still common in the country for all kinds of foods.

Though some people in snow country have opted for plastic sheets to cover ground floor windows and walls in the winter, the traditional snow protectors of reed stalks are still much favored. Sometimes the traditional way is more satisfying and may even work better than clever plastic.

Tradition Reborn

Some twenty years ago, a young man from Tokyo saw the cover of a Japanese country life magazine and decided that this was the way he wanted to live. The cover featured three people on the porch of a simple, one-story thatched farmhouse. Nothing fancy, but somehow it called to the twenty-year-old Kenji Tsuchisawa, who has a way of making dreams materialize.

On the border of Tochigi and Ibaraki prefectures, tucked into the hills at the end of seven kilometers of winding dirt farm road, Tsuchisawa-san discovered a hopelessly derelict farmhouse by the side of a rice field that was being allowed to

quietly biodegrade back into the environment. Amazingly, serendipitously, it turned out to be in the next town over from the house he had seen on the magazine cover. Though he suspected the house was beyond rescue, he bought it and started on the long road back to restoring it. The roof needed repair urgently, and luckily there were thatchers nearby who were able to restore the distinctive topping of golden reeds peculiar to that area. White plaster now covers the walls between dark brown wooden beams and supports, and strangely enough, the lovely Japanese style garden as you turn the corner into the

front, gives the house almost the air of a pastoral English country cottage.

From the outside, the house has not been altered much except for the aluminum sashes and screens that are necessary concessions to winter winds and summer bugs. But the atmosphere is unchanged, and the wooden sliding doors and checkerboard window covers produce a playful surface of contrasting patterns. The coupling of the carpenters' skill with functional design makes for an interesting surface design.

The house is fronted with windows and sliding doors in such a way that only sliding paper shoji screens stand between inside and outside. A slab of wood built into the wall at the entrance with a chair in front cleverly uses available space in an unobtrusive way and invites us to sit down and write our notes, use the telephone, even pay our bills. Next to it a charming chest holds all the necessities of the house—glasses and cups on the top behind sliding doors, and a multitude of drawers storing everything from tablecloths and napkins to scissors and tape. Beside it is the door to the kitchen, semiconcealed by a hemp half-curtain (*noren*). In the corner at the back sits a cozy built-in

table covered with a tablecloth of indigo kasuri. One of the real nuisances of going inside and outside of Japanese houses, country or otherwise, is the need to keep putting shoes on and off, particularly if they happen to be laced, or worse still, boots, a natural choice for the country. Kenji Tsuchisawa has eliminated this trouble by paving

the old earthen-floored entry/work area of the house with flagstones, thus making it a shoes-on zone, for kitchen, writing and eating and sitting areas. It also means that the tatami-matted raised portion of the house floor becomes a resting area, where you sit to take off your shoes or just sit to enjoy the view. Somehow the small house works out to be ingeniously convenient and answers the simple needs of everyday living. You do not spend a lot of time deciding whether to put shoes on or off. It works beautifully even when going in and out again and again.

As you step out of your shoes and up into the main section of the house to a large open floor with an irori in the center, the high beams and the soaring ceiling of straw—the underside of the thatch—immediately catch your eye, adding to the great feeling of warmth and

texture and comfort found in natural materials. The carefree chaos of the tucks of straw disarms you as you sit around the irori hearth over tea or a game of go. A wooden staircase with a burnished caramel candy cane of a bannister leads up to a loft with a

48

perch for surveying the scene below and the ceiling above. Here one can just sit and observe, or tuck into one of the futon stashed away for visitors, secure between the charming ceiling and the beams that play in space. Flexible, adaptable, open space—one of the most precious elements of the Japanese country house—is used here to great advantage and answers the basic needs for comfort and convenience and beauty in country living. Slatted doors behind the hearth area open to reveal a large expanse of tatami furnished sparely with a chest, whose two sections have been separated and placed side by side. Futon in the closet can make this room into a bedroom or sitting room or whatever is needed. The abundance of space and the number of uses for this small house generate energy and surprise, as unexpected uses appear in unexpected ways. All who come here are delighted by the flexibilty and energy that this unimposing country cottage, restored by a man with a dream, creates.

Top right: The irori is an open hearth where people gather to warm themselves, to drink tea, and eat. A kettle is constantly kept boiling over a charcoal fire. Pothooks (jizai-kagi) are often decorated with a fish in wood or metal.
Left and far left: Different views of the main living area of Kenji Tsuchisawa's house.
Top left: The view through the open door of the Tsuchisawa house.

The *Genkan*

The genkan, or entranceway, is the place where the inside and outside meet. The floor once was of packed earth, though now stone and concrete are usual. Shoes, boots, and the outside mind are shed in the genkan, and slippers await everyone who makes that conscious step up into the house itself. Thus shod in socks and slippers, visitors and family alike are equally exposed and vulnerable.

The decoration of the genkan varies with the house. Flowers of season may be arranged in a basket, welcoming the visitor and recalling nature outside. A noren, or split curtain, is often used as a delicate delineator of space. In the spacious genkan of inns and large houses, a single-panel standing screen is often used to define the inner from the outer and break the space in an attractive and interesting way. The entryway is also a challenge to the architect. In the contemporary country house pictured here, the genkan shows an artistic use of earth and stone on the floor and of weathered timbers to frame a door.

50

Top: The inner garden of the Yoyokaku Inn in Karatsu, Kyushu, a lovely example of sophisticated country taste. Above: Flowers brighten the gate pictured on opposite page.

Choosing Country

I have met many people living in country houses and opting for the country spirit, and have always tried to find out why. One consistent element I have noticed is that people who have left the city in favor of the countryside have lived or traveled abroad, or even married someone from abroad. Distance seems to give a fresh perspective on the traditions of Japan. With love and attention, houses once considered old-fashioned and dirty regain dignity and respect. Looking at traditional Japan from a step removed lets one see what amazing creations even the simpler country houses are, made by country carpenters with few tools—saw, ax, adz, mortising chisels, plumb line—available materials, and unlimited resourcefulness and skill.

Above and left: The exterior is a silent adjunct to Japanese interiors, made more noticeable by the use of large sliding doors and windows. Inside and outside flow into each other, creating new perspectives. As the genkan bids you enter up into the house, so the concept of *oku*, the deep interior, draws you into the inner sanctum of the house.

Tradition Redefined

Tucked in against the hills in a mountain farming village north of Kyoto is an unpretentious house topped with a shiny black corrugated roof that protects the thick layer of thatch beneath. Tools of living and working are scattered and hung with a tidy nonchalance that gives no indication of the order and pursuit of beauty within. In 1979, Douglas Woodruff and his effervescent wife, Kiyo, moved out to the countryside of Kyoto, where houses were mostly thatched and machines had not yet come to the rice fields, nor concrete to the riverbanks. They found a charming, stately country house and decided to live in its generous space and nurse it back to good health and well-being after years of neglect. While preserving the character of the house, they have worked to establish their own way of life.

At the side of the earthen-floored entryway (left) is a massive *kamado* (above), a black clay cooking stove. Smoke-blackened beams play in the high spaces overhead. The

Previous page: The earthen doma floor is alive—in the wet season, moss grows on the bumpy surface, which changes with the seasons. The kamado stove was sited to be accessible both from the work area and the raised floor of the house.

Above: In the Woodruff kitchen, there is no pretense, only utility.
Right: A folk figure graces the lid of an old rice-cooking pot.
Far right: Douglas and Kiyo Woodruff chat over an impromptu Sunday lunch.

Following pages: The *kotatsu*, a small covered table with a heating element underneath, invites everyone to tuck their legs under the quilt for toe-to-toe conversations.

outside working world comes right to where the dirt floor ends; with the high step up onto the tatami, the living quarters begin. Directly behind the kamado is a kitchen dotted with eye-catching accents—lovely glaze-dripped pots of sugar, jam, and mustard, a picture of the zodiac animal of the year, various flea-market finds—and an ingenuous kitchen table that divides the narrow space gracefully.

The table is Douglas's creation. He has supported one edge of a slab of marble with an old ladder laid on its side and made a one-of-a-kind piece of furniture. He specializes in recycling old pieces of wood and not only brings them back to life with his patience and skill, but injects them with new vigor and purpose.

"Why not use traditional things in new ways?" claims Doug. "They are made to be used. Old lifestyles change, and old uses are no longer needed. Why can't we adapt them to new needs, new ways of living?" A wooden platform off the living room extends outside into the garden, where we have coffee and talk in the presence of the hills behind, its denizens, birdsong, and a stately old tree. A skylight brings extra light into an essentially dark house.

(to page 60)

Both Woodruffs scour flea markets and antique shops in search of beautiful things to add to their life. They call this "sparking," coming up with their own new ideas and thoughts, sparked by the energy of the old crafts and yesterday's beauty that they unearth. "There is only one person living here," admits Douglas. Completely attuned, they have chosen everything in the house together. Horses and rabbits are favored motifs because they are their respective zodiac animals.

Tables Douglas has crafted are pieces of derelict wood provided by a thatcher and

house restorer nearby. Smooth, mellow pieces of love and sweat, intelligence and patience, each is the individual answer and response of a woodworker to his materials. Using his own house as a reference and source of inspiration, he searches for new ways of taking old pieces of wood and recrafting them into tables for today. He seeks to keep the spirit of the wood vital and inspiring for people looking for living furniture in these days of mindless and heartless designer objects.

The outhouse is part of the barn, which consists of several stalls, decked with baskets of flowers and hemp horse trappings with a rabbit design hung on the wall.

Beside them is the spacious bathroom, which houses a smooth, round bathtub (see photo page 91) that is wood-fired from the outside. During the autumn and winter, Douglas lights it before dinner, to make the water as hot as possible so that it will cool to a comfortable temperature for a sustaining and warming bath before going to bed.

Simply turning on the hot water and adding more is not an option in this basic country arrangement, nor is carefree relaxation. It requires dedicated work and wise planning —not to mention enthusiasm—to keep the household system running smoothly.

The Woodruffs have worked hard to blend history and the present in this house, which is more a member of the family than a possession. Besides the constant surprises of old objects, carefully chosen and arranged in unusual ways, there is a microwave oven hidden in an old kitchen chest and a computer workstation in a study built into a loft space accessible by ladder.

Above: Tea in the Uchida house, under a textured ceiling.
Opposite: Smoke from the wood-burning stove in the Shindo house circulates above the ceiling and beneath the rafters, where it keeps roof bindings taut and thatch dry.

62

Previous page: For a city dweller,
cooking with wood on a Japanese
kamado stove is labor intensive,
but offers a challenge and
satisfaction. An American wood-
burner with oven is at far left, and
a stoneware water storage jar is
in the foreground at far right.

66

Left: The traditional hearth (*irori*) harmonizes beautifully with the needs of a modern family. In the Umesao family kitchen, a counter provides a convenient place for quick meals. In the right foreground is a well-kept irori, with its iron pot suspended above. Below: A traditional kitchen chest is the ideal place for storing a collection of blue-and-white bowls and dishes, and some colorful woven *obi*.

Opposite page, right: An impressive English table seats fifteen workers or visitors to the kiln of artist-potter Takashi Nakazato outside of Karatsu, Kyushu. Nakazato fully utilizes the interior of his country home in his constant search for ways to make his vessels useful.
Left: The graceful entranceway of the Nakazato house.
Below: A massive slab of wood serves as a table in the living room of the Umesao house. Nothing extraneous is used. The basic forms and shapes, the oversized Noguchi lantern, the table, the chest—all give the room tremendous strength. The moss garden at back is newly redesigned by landscape artist Marc Keane.

Left: The Nakazato house irori seen from straight-on.
Following pages: The main room at Sanso Murata. Completed in 1992, Sanso Murata is a unique inn—a collection of eight folk houses from different parts of Japan filled with modern Western art. The man responsible is Koji Fujibayashi, who has mixed traditional country architecture and contemporary western art in an original and exciting new country style.

The Art of Display

A Japanese folk house is a wonderful venue for displaying art, but the house itself sets high and exacting standards for the objects that are brought into it. The strength of character of the house and its essential honesty will reveal any weakness, shallowness, or sham in objects—antique or contemporary. Almost any kind of object, even baroque furniture, is possible, but it first must undergo the demanding scrutiny of the house before it becomes part of one's life. Where else can one find such a precise and eloquent art critic, and without using words?

Top: A large nineteenth-century chest in the Woodruff house. Bottom: An art lover in a remote valley in the Noto Peninsula owns this screen of mundane creatures—bullocks and birds.

Top: A very stylish, polished irori, beyond which lies a colorful kilim rug.

Bottom: A naif indigo *tsutsugaki* futon cover with a crane and turtle motif hung on an old loom for making straw mats.

Top: Art on the walls makes a simple entranceway warm and inviting.

Bottom: A fine indigo sleeping kimono on a traditional stand is art enough to beautify a small tatami room.

Above: Beauty in small places brings comfort and warmth to the daily activities of life. The items on this dresser—the vase, the old mirror with drawer for whatnots, the small porcelain dishes—and the indigo tsutsu-gaki child's futon are all beautiful crafts of a past that is all too often ignored today.

Above: Beauty and comfort are created in a Japanese room by understatement. Furnishings and objects are kept to a minimum. A padded kimono is used as the quilt, or upper futon; two halves of a chest are placed side-by-side; tea things are set out for a sip before sleeping; and a tsutsugaki wall hanging adds grace.

Opposite page: Old country things and modern living. In this rebuilt farmhouse in Karuizawa, an old weathered sleigh fitted with indigo-covered cushions makes an unusual seat.

This page, left center: A straw snow boot holds flowers in front of an antique tsutsugaki textile.

Left top: A wooden tofu mold used as a flower container.

Left bottom: A section of an old water wheel holds slippers.

Below: Conventional edging for tatami mats has here been replaced with pieces of old blue-and-white *kasuri* kimono.

Preceding pages: Shown are the animal quarters of an old house, which has been fitted with cushions covered in indigo for sitting and reading or having tea. A ladder gives access to the upper levels, where silkworms once were kept, and the family now sleeps.

Above: A folk textile is a backdrop for a Japanese chest on which are a newly papered lantern (*andon*), the equipment for papering it (scissors, glue, paper, brush), and an old roof tile in the form of a crane, which echoes the motif in the textile. Opposite: The lantern is lit by a traditional Japanese candle, whose spindle shape is made to be supported on a spike. These candles are handmade of vegetable wax, refined from the berries of the wax tree or lacquer tree, and have a paper wick, which burns with a clear, steady light.

Restoring an Old House

Country folk houses were built for utility, not for beauty or comfort. Restoring an old house allows its intrinsic beauty to be brought out, and makes it more comfortable. Furnishing and appointing such a house in a manner true to the spirit of the original and yet respecting the needs of today is not easy. It takes years of picking and choosing and taking into consideration not only your own taste, but also that of the house, which has clear likes and dislikes. On bringing something into the house, it is not long before you know whether it goes or not, be it an antique lamp, an unusual textile, or even a portable telephone. When integrating possessions from various eras into a *minka* (country house), one must ask what kind of furniture fits into the great rooms. What kind of sleeping arrangements work under old beams that once overlooked baskets of silk worms noisily eating mulberry leaves?

Left: Bedrooms can take many forms in country houses. Here they are austere tatami-matted rooms that have been transformed into cozy nests by piles of futon pulled out of the bedding closet in the evening before bedtime.

Above: An inviting bedroom in the Sanso Murata inn, Yufuin, Kyushu, successfully blends colorful Tiffany lamps and goosedown quilts with the white plaster and dark beams of a renovated country house.

Below Left: A *sashiko* fisherman's coat on the wall overlooks twin beds covered with patched quilts.
Below right: An antique tsutsugaki futon cover gives character to a modern bed nestled under the beams of a cozy country house.

Above left: Every room needs a stack of square *zabuton* floor cushions, here of contemporary kasuri, to put to use anytime, anywhere.
Above right: The bright colors and bold graphics of a fisherman's banner, here used as a bedcover, give energy to a teenage boy's room.
Opposite: A stair chest (*kaidan-dansu*) is used as it was intended, for storage and as stairs, in this case to the cozy bedroom at top.

Above: The modern approach to traditional country architecture brings as much light as possible into the house.

Left: The joys of country living—interesting reading, afternoon sunshine, and a window full of autumn grasses in a contemporary house that captures the spirit of the traditional.

Opposite page, left: Tree-lined steps with a graceful bamboo railing lead up to a country cottage built on a hill.

Opposite page, right: A peaceful, sunny room with a well-used armchair and a view of a restful bamboo grove.

The weighty and expensive materials of old folk houses are not the popular choice of the house-owning public, but there are still those who opt for their spirit and style. Juxtapositions of dark beams, plaster, and tile reveal the honest work of carpenter and plasterer and give a ring of truth to the interior and the traditional way of living. ◼

The Bath

The *ofuro* (bath) is for cleanliness, and cleanliness is almost the same as godliness in Japan. There is a stage of enlightenment that comes in the bath in Japan, and so the room and its appointments are given special reverence. Only

the best materials are used. Special windows are sometimes built to offer scenic views of the outside to the reclining bather. Country inns and spas pride themselves on their bath architecture, and many books and guides have been published about Japan's rock-filled, waterfalled, thatched and beam-ceilinged kingdoms for cleansing mind and body. The making of wooden bathtubs is a highly skilled craft, and the bathub craftsman also makes the little wooden buckets, the stools for squatting while you wash, and the long-handled device for churning the scalding water.

The bath is so valued in Japanese culture that the size of the room tends to be large when compared with, say, the kitchen. It is here where everyone ends the day and soaks away cares and worries. Here there is rebirth.

Right: The innkeeper's private bath at the Kame no Ii inn (inset above) at Yufuin, Kyushu, a luxurious resort hotel with thatched bathhouses and a modern craft shop.

Outdoor Baths

One of the most exquisite forms of bathing is the *rotenburo*, the open-air bath. In Japan, such idylls are usually nestled in quiet scenic places, with the sound of water running down rocks into the pool. In more active hot-spring areas, the hot water does indeed spring from the ground. Rotenburo are found by riverbanks and by the sea, wherever a hot-spring has chosen to emerge.

Opposite page: A private rotenburo was built by the owner of a restored folk house on a bluff overlooking the Pacific Ocean south of Tokyo so he could sit and contemplate nature and his house.
Top: One of the serene baths at the Kame no Ii inn in Kyushu.
Above: The wood-fired bath in the Woodruff house.
Left: An old package of bath salts graphically depicts the heat and steam to be found at a traditional Japanese hot spring.

Country Character

For too long, "country" was for bumpkins, and the best and brightest people left the rural areas for the city. This trend seems to be reversing. The young couple pictured above left trendy, urban jobs to live outside Wajima, in the Noto Peninsula, where he apprenticed to a become a lacquer craftsman and she raised two children. After five years, the Akagi family has built a small house designed by a local architect who specializes in artistic use of local materials.

Opposite page: A cigarette break under a temple bell. This page, clockwise from top: The Akagi family, the family goat, shoes in the genkan, and the house, under construction.

Country clothing was made for work, and indigo was the color of work clothes. Women, always careful to protect their heads from the sun by wrapping in towels, become lumpy bundles of activity working in the fields or by the roadside. The once common *mompe*, the baggy, indigo women's work pants, are now considered embarrassingly old-fashioned and have been largely replaced by nondescript trousers.

Clothing

The design of the traditional Japanese kimono was largely determined by the standard width of the loom, which was based on the width of the human body. Though the kimono is basically a two-dimensional garment, there was a great deal of variation.

With country clothes, sleeves were made to give freedom of arm motion; pants for men were shin-hugging, and women wore the baggy mompe. Belts and obi, often colorful ragweaves, secured both jacket and kimono. Individual flourishes and differences came with territory, climate, and tradition. A student of the subject can look at the pants shape, the jacket, and particularly the head wrapping and know where the costume came from and what it was used for.

Opposite page, top: Nature follows art. The harvest motif of cranes and rice on this exuberant sleeping kimono is echoed by the rice hung to dry on racks in a field; middle: Examples of country footwear and the wooden lasts used to make them; bottom: Festival jackets and the traditional *tenugui* (handtowels) twisted and tied jauntily around the heads of boys before a festival in Karatsu. This page, left: Vintage postcard of a country girl. Note footwear.

Above: An old advertisement for tea. The tea-picker wears a bold kasuri kimono.
Left: Calligrapher and artist Hisako Hagiwara has her own, unconventional style of wearing kimono and obi. Here her kimono is a kind of sashiko, stitched with thick, colored thread.

Markets

Whether it is a morning market such as at Wajima and Takayama or a monthly flea market or an annual pottery market, whether what is being sold is fish just off the boat, pickles, antique porcelains, used kimono, cheap socks, or five mushrooms and two turnips, a market has something special that touches us and an energy that reaffirms our humanity. When people gather to buy and sell the best there is at the time, the earth spins a little faster. Japanese markets are not really different from markets elsewhere, except for the things sold, but the market is one of the few occasions in Japan when spontaneity and openness rule, and the only social distinctions are between buyer and seller.

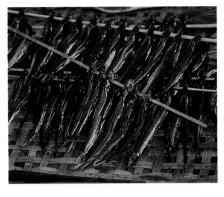

Though now a self-conscious tourist attraction, the morning market in Wajima still provides the community with what is fresh. Women from the fishing port and farmers' wives bring whatever is in season, directly from boat or garden or forest. Crowds of local people mingle with visitors as children pass on their way to school. The sellers call out the virtues of their wares, and bargaining voices add to the general bustle.

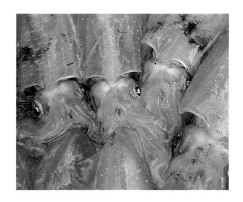

As well, dried, pickled, and preserved fish and other seafoods and seaweeds, wild mushrooms and tubers, medicinal barks, twigs and herbs, beans and seeds, plants and flowers demand attention. The market is held in any weather, and when it closes at noon, the women put the remaining fresh fish or produce in a cart or mini-pickup truck and make the rounds of houses and villages in the district.

Above: A felicitous textile sculpture by Harue Takami is hung in the Umesao house to help celebrate the new year. Below: A *torii* (gate) guards the entrance to a mountain shrine.

Spirit and Belief

You are never far from a sense of the spiritual in the Japanese countryside. Shinto is basically animistic—mountains, trees, rocks, waterfalls, natural formations are imbued with spirit, with the sacred. The land itself is inhabited by the deities of nature. Shinto shrines and Buddhist temples are surrounded by ancient trees. Roadside shrines are ubiquitous, and at a bend in a country path or under an overhang, there may be a stone image or two—perhaps a Jizo (guardian saint of small children) with a red bib or, in the central mountains, Dosojin, the twin deities of the road. Set in a hilly slope or a garden may be a miniature shrine to the God of the Mountains with a stone sphere on its altar—all of which show that this is a countryside in which something godly is very much present.

The crafts have always been a major interface between the sacred and the material world. This was once true everywhere, but in Japan it is still true in many ways. The craftsman respects and honors the inner qualities of his materials, his tools, and, by extension, of all materials and art. The act of making something is a recognition of processes and forces larger than, or at least different from, the merely human.

Opposite: A creative—yet traditional—New Year's still life. A rabbit made of rice cake with ears of bamboo leaves perches along with a citron atop a folded stack of seaweed in the Hagiwara house, in Totsuka, near Yokohama.

The festival is a celebration of season usually with agricultural origins, when the god of a shrine comes down off his altar and man pays his respects. Sometimes the deity is carried through the streets of city, town, and hamlet in a portable shrine. The variety and number of such observances throughout Japan—fire festivals, lantern festivals, some with processions, some with sacred dances— never cease to amaze me. Festivals in the country are vital community events, participated in with energy and sincerity and very much a part of the yearly cycle of life and belief.

Opposite top: A household shrine overlooking a craftsman's workplace. Opposite bottom: Symbolic decorations for a roof-raising celebration. Above: A demonic mask hung on the main pillar of a house protects the household. Left: An elderly woman praying before a Shinto shrine.

A festival is a celebration, a reveling in life, and a welcoming of the presence of the gods. It is a time of transformation, through intricate ritual in the shrine, in household observances, in community festivities, and in music and dance. The people taking part in the festival become messengers of the gods and are imbued with the sacred. Dancers often wear masks, which transport them and the spectators to another world, where the mundane is abandoned. And to seal the compact with the divine, no festival is complete without an abundance of good food and drink.

This page and opposite: Hiroji Hashimoto, a doll maker of Miharu, has become famous for keeping alive various country dance celebrations, including the Seven Gods of Good Fortune *(Shichifukujin)* dance pictured here.

THE ART OF EVERYDAY

Novelist Jun'ichiro Tanizaki in his incisive book on Japanese aesthetics, *In Praise of Shadows*, remarks that indigenous Japanese solutions to problems of life were unique and unlike those of the West. Had Japan not been opened to the West, those solutions might still be offering to the world fresh, alternative ways of doing and making things.

This observation holds true for country living in Japan. Distinctive and regional ways of doing things resulted in a marriage of the sensitive use of material and the function intended. In a time before "design" was deified and worshipped in marble chapels of learning, country farmers and their wives, carpenters and plasterers were creating rich and powerful tools for everyday life out of the materials they found around them.

Designs came from a close relationship with nature and were decided by the combining of materials, techniques, and usage. When little was available, country ingenuity conjured up practical solutions to the problems of living. The directness and simplicity of such everyday solutions often amazes us today, as we rely on technology and industry to supply the answers.

The pantry, or cooler, beneath the kitchen floor (page 112, top) is a traditional feature of Japanese house design still often included in modern dwellings. A small wooden box tacked up just inside the entranceway may be used for letters or for needed tools—here (page 112), a pair of iron garden snippers. Panels and sliding doors are easily locked with a length of bamboo (page 113, bottom) appropriately wedged into a corner. Such creative answers to everyday problems produced objects whose direct and vital forms remain inspirations to designers today.

The tree was one of man's first friends for building shelter, for making tools, for crafting things for living. A close physical bond with nature as well as a spiritual bond with the gods of the forests gave carpenters and woodworkers insight into the soul of the tree, its nature and disposition. Wood was

considered a living thing with a soul, and the way of the carpenter was to keep that soul alive. The carpenter's appreciation of the shape and grain and texture of the wood was at the heart of each object he made.

Next to the tree, the earth itself was man's most commonly used material. Walls, floors, pots, dishes, cooking stoves, roofing tiles—earth was put to a wide variety of different uses, by itself or transmuted by fire. Earth was integral to the Japanese farmhouse in a huge variety of ways long forgotten by the West. Packed, it formed the floor of the work area/entrance; laced with straw and slathered over bamboo latticework, it formed the wattle and daub walls of the house; combined with tiles, themselves created of earth, it made cooking stoves.

Clay is earth, and from the very earliest times, man has known how to marry clay and fire for making vessels for cooking and eating. In clay as in wood, Japanese crafts-men have been in sympathy with both the nature of the material and the objects made. Throughout history these highly skilled artisans have constantly made efforts to use a material in the most natural way, to send it even further, as it were, along the same path it was already travel-ing. The result has always been distinct regional answers to the true nature of the clay and the needs of the area—straightforward, functional beauty.

Stones were the dwelling places of the gods and were used largely unchanged in building supports under pillars to keep them from rotting in a wet climate. Stones with special shapes were prized in the garden, and hollowed-out stones were used for basins outside as well as other devices for working, grinding, and cooking inside the house as well as out. Man cleverly, sensitively, diplomatically followed the dictates of nature and used the stones he found in the way nature suggested.

Bamboo was the most flexible country resource, the one that most did what man asked. It is one of the great pillars of Japanese country life. Its strength, flexibility, and the fact that it replenishes itself, makes it suitable for practically any task. From walls and ceilings, to tools for working and eating, to baskets and tea whisks, there is no country house that can function without bamboo. It was the all-purpose material—supplanted now by plastic —without which people could not have survived. And it was part of the nature of survival that every man and woman had basic skills for crafting bamboo.

Paper was another essential of daily life. It was used to cover screens and doors, to kept out the cold and let in the light. It was even used in weaving clothes and reinforcing baskets, and mending broken windows and jars. Saved and reused time again, paper has been a faithful and invaluable servant in country life.

Above: Homemade New Year's decorations are an important facet of family life in the countryside. Here, they add a touch of whimsy to a dark living room corner.
Opposite: Eclectic and seemingly unrelated objects often make captivating displays. In this case, a giant wooden mortar, an old fishing boat's running light, and a basket sieve suffice to decorate the genkan of a rented farmhouse.

Above: Fresh, crisp, pickled vegetables from the garden often accompany afternoon tea in the countryside. Here a large, smooth river rock weights a small wooden tub of pickled cabbage. Right: A red lacquered bucket ingeniously transformed into an unusual speaker enclosure.

Buckets and Tubs

The cooper was a skilled and important craftsman in traditional country life. Anything from huge casks for brewing saké and miso tubs and buckets used around the farm to special vessels for kitchen use required his deft hand. Bathtubs were made and repaired by a cooper specializing in making these and associated objects, which required a somewhat different set of skills and knowledge of the special woods used.

Where the Western cooper holds barrels and tubs together with metal hoops, the Japanese craftsman generally employs wide, plaited strips of bamboo for this purpose.

Many types of Japanese food, including a wide variety of pickled foods enjoyed throughout the country, have no counterpart in the West. Almost all of this pickling was done in the barrels and tubs produced by the cooper.

Arrangements

The best arrangements of country things just happen—unplanned, undesigned, natural accidents of placement of what is used around the house. Sometimes this becomes hopeless clutter without a saving virtue. But, then, if the gods are smiling, the litter of living can have tremendous appeal, precisely because it is not arranged or thought out. It comes directly from country traditions of having what is necessary and nothing extra. Things are put

where they should be, and they are where they are for a reason. Even their storage can have beauty because it is unaffected and nothing is hidden. Sense of purpose was a basic part of traditional country living. A certain thing was made for a certain job, and usually that also entailed a container or a box or a place where it was stored. There was a strong sense of appropriateness, of order and of place, which we could learn from today. The containers can still create a sense of order and beauty in the helter-skelter of our modern-day lives.

Top: Dried rice is stored on poles above the entrance to a craftsman's work area.
Middle: Cups on a table and *yuzu* citrons form a beautiful, spontaneous still life.
Bottom: A collection of unusual *geta* clogs fills a genkan.
Opposite: A little Japanese pot-bellied stove is the center of winter life in Hisako Hagiwara's house. In her life, there is no division between her collections and her artistic creations.

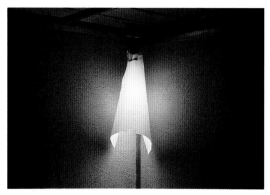

Lighting

Lighting in country houses was generally a home-grown affair. Each household devised its own solutions to needs for lighting using the materials available—bamboo, paper, wood, and occasionally iron. The results were original pieces of ingenuity, fortuitously seasoned with a twist of humor, a spot of the unexpected, and a dab of beauty.

Opposite top: A section of bamboo, cut out and covered with Japanese paper, becomes a clever light. Other photos: Every space has its own character, calling for a special lighting solution, be it bamboo, wood, iron, or paper.

Beauty in unnoticed places: the eye is drawn to forms and arrangements and colors in the country, from bicycles hung on a wall to a patchwork quilt of old handtowels saved over the years to straw-bound branches used as tripods for hanging rice at harvest time, from a simple sink to a washbasin made of an old imari bowl, from a tidy woodpile to a traditional duster made of torn strips of paper to artistic electric wiring left bare for all to see in a contemporary country house.

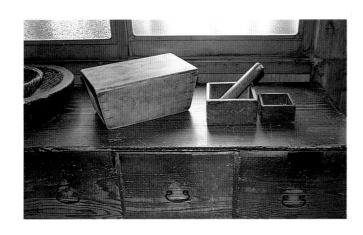

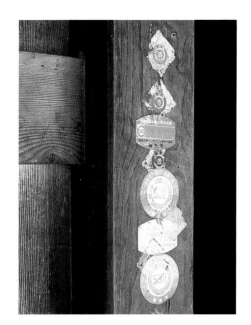

Sign Language. The muted browns and grays and ecrus of country buildings make all colored signs, advertisements, posters and the like, no matter how mundane, seem like wild shouts of color.

Opposite: The plaster policeman once sufficed for patrolling country roads. Today, he and his cohorts are relegated to a junkyard cemetery, although from time to time, he can still be found standing guard at dangerous intersections.

Collections

Collections are a small way of grasping at the infinite. By bringing together a number of one kind of thing, you begin to glimpse something much larger. The small collection—no more than a few examples of something—gives a kind of satisfaction quite different from owning a single object. The whole is much larger than each part. The major collection is a microcosm of something vast and expansive.

Putting the discards of the past and of another culture to use in our own life is a real challenge and a creative act. In some cases, the object's original function cries out to be honored. The traditional marriage of function and form is a key concept of handmade articles and one we should all appreciate and learn from. So take whatever treasure you find and ascertain its original function. Use it that way, if possible, or, use it in a new way.

Life today has changed drastically from the times in which many of these finds were made, so we would also do well to find new work for the old pieces that attract us. It gives great pleasure to reuse something in a new and dynamic manner—with a bit of imagination and experimentation, an object's usefulness can be stretched. This is not hard to do with old Japanese things, because we are not using them as they were intended anyway. (to page 130)

Right: Votive pictures (*ema*) from temples and shrines often depict the Chinese zodiacal animals.

Far left: Favorite things carefully chosen, tastefully arranged. A variety of antique blue-and-white sauce cups for eating *soba* noodles please both the eye and the soul.

Left: A small set of shelves in the *tokonoma* alcove is filled with old Imari cups and a sashiko tea towel. Overhead, a tangle of wild wisteria fibers replaces the conventional flower arrangement.

Groupings by utility may be more effective than carefully planned one-of-a-kind displays.
Far left: Kitchen baskets and measures in a kitchen at the Shiramine Outdoor Museum of Folk Houses.
Left: Brooms and baskets in a modern working kitchen.

Far left: Sweets from the kitchen of a confectioner in Karatsu are an art in themselves, almost too beautiful to eat.
Left: Sample pottery cups by potter Tessai Hirakawa show various glazes.

A personal collection of unmatched tea bowls in front of a *shoji* screen lattice makes an interesting composition.

An assortment of traditional, handmade geta entice the eye in a country shoe shop.

Visitors to the second-floor of Wajima's Tefu Tefu shop can choose glasses and saké cups from a selection of fine pieces.

A tatami maker's entranceway reveals who has come to lunch.

A selection of stripes for all seasons, for men and for horses.

In Hita, Oita Prefecture, one shop leaves footwear for people to take or trade as they stroll through the streets.

Both one-of-a-kind things and collections give great satisfaction. If you like one thing, and it says something to you, with three like objects, the statement is stronger. Somewhere after acquiring six similar things, a collection is born. And with it comes the sense that you are collecting something unlike anyone else. It has something of you in it, your taste, your way of seeing and appreciating the world around you. In some way it helps define you, gives you a creative and imaginative dimension while feeding a passion. As you continue collecting and displaying, the passion grows. Displaying a collection is a vital way to brighten up a corner or make a larger statement in your house while providing that daily dose of beauty, without which, for me anyway, living is incomplete.

Opposite top: Foxes, messengers of the gods, are made as amulets at shrines. This collection includes both old and new figures.

Opposite bottom: A woodblock cat amulet from Hakkaizan Shrine in Yamata Machi in Niigata prefecture keeps mice away.

Above: In the eighteenth and nineteenth centuries, as today, sumo wrestlers were popular heroes. Until the early part of this century, woodblock prints of sumo wrestlers were cut out and used as card games.

Left: A small fox figure stands guard at the window of a country house.

THE REFINED JAPANESE SAKE

KOZUKA JYOZOJYO

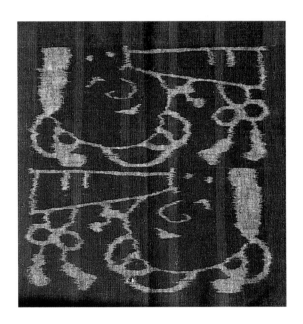

Otafuku Charm. Detractors who accuse Japan of being a faceless society, a nation with no wit and less jollity, must meet Otafuku. Fat cheeks, snub nose, rosebud mouth, tiny dabs of eyebrows, homely Otafuku keeps on smiling. The principal at fertility rites and many country festivals, Otafuku is a symbol to the people of the good woman and mother. She is no beauty, but she is the one you depend on to love, comfort, and protect.

In traditional Japan, she was an archetypal figure of wide popularity, found in the folk art of the city as well as the country. Each Otafuku was different, each an original harbinger of goodwill, an invocation of good fortune. To generations of Japanese, she embodied the proverb *Warau kado fuku kitaru*—"Fortune comes to the house full of laughter."

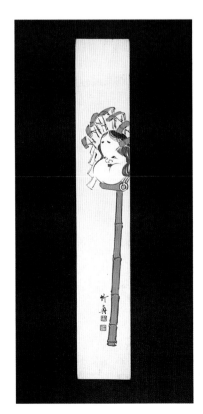

Striking steps into the modern age, household matches were an early export from a newly industrialized Japan toward the end of the nineteenth century. The label designs, whether auspicious rabbits or turtles or

134

mythical figures or common household items, were originally spinoffs of woodblock print artists. Collectibles today, these miniature works of art and their designs of traditional figures reach deep into country beliefs.

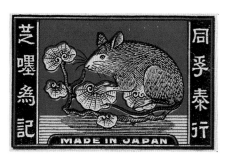

Materials and Makers

In Japan there is a certain insistence on beauty in all craftwork. Stated another way, the connection between rural Japan's material world and spiritual world was traditionally in the crafts. Things made by hand were first and foremost offerings to the gods in true and sincere acts of belief. Deep within these honest works is a piety and devotion that speaks out to me as I look at them, or, better still, live with them.

But country crafts also answered the needs of every-

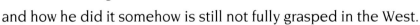

day living; they were practical, as well as beautiful, just as the gods, who oversaw all of man's activities, were gods of practicality.

The Japanese craftsman has been sufficiently romanticized, but the essential message of what he did and how he did it somehow is still not fully grasped in the West.

Simply, the Japanese craftsman *allowed* materials to speak directly. This does not mean sloppy work or lackadaisical technique, or a surrender to natural forces. To the

contrary, the Japanese craftsman had awesome knowledge of technique and used it with power and equally awesome skill. This might better be called wisdom, the kind that comes from direct, personal experience and that is compiled from the instinct and experience of gen-

erations of craftsmen—that is, from that power source called tradition. The country potter dug his own clay and knew in intimate detail just how to refine and age it according to its nature, to form and trim the pot, and how to fire it—in what part of the kiln to put that specific type and shape of pot; he knew the exact color of the fire and pot surface when the ware matures at the height of the firing. This knowledge was all directed toward the single aim of making the pot be totally itself, of letting clay and glaze (if any) and decoration all work together while each keeps its own identity. Decoration, in fact, was often considered to be just an effect of forming or firing. The same degree of involvement and wisdom is found in all traditional, and some modern, Japanese handwork, whether it is simply making a straw rope, weaving a basket, building a house, creating the joinery for a table, or the involved and labor-intensive community-craft of fine lacquerwork. The world of crafts in Japan is a kingdom unto itself that has provided articles of daily living with a consistently high level of beauty. For me, Japanese crafts talk straight, direct, and true, but from the

entire body—from the bones out rather than from just the neck up. The same kind of process is present in making bamboo baskets (right), ceramic vessels (above), elaborate roof-ridge tiles finials (top) and in creating a table of bleached and weathered ship timbers (opposite top). At the very heart of this is the craftsman's faith and his respect for the natural, god-given materials that connect man to his sources.

137

Papier-mâché toys made of many layers of handmade, *washi* paper applied over solid wooden molds have been part of traditional country Japan for centuries. Legendary heroes, characters from fairy tales, and religious figures are all found in the lively doll tradition. Doll making was introduced in the early eighteenth century to the town of Miharu, Fukushima Prefecture, by the local lord to educate people while encouraging a cottage industry, and it is still lively today. The tradition is preserved in the massive folk house of Hiroji Hashimoto, a seventeenth-generation toymaker whose toys have a particular spontaneity of line and freshness of color, for which the Miharu dolls are justly famous.

Washi

Papermaking was one of the great rural crafts. Most papermakers were farmers who used the winter months to supplement income from crops with this labor-intensive, demanding craft. A century ago, there were thousands of papermaking households throughout Japan, and the variety and quality of papers produced have never been surpassed, except, perhaps, by the gold-decorated papers made by the imperial court paper mill about nine hundred years ago. Paper mulberry (*kozo*) and the plants called *mitsumata* and *gampi* provided the main paper fibers. Mulberry is the tough, masculine fiber, producing papers that have been used in every aspect of daily life and that have lasted centuries without apparent change, varying in thickness from boards to gossamer-like filter papers for lacquer. Mitsumata paper is the blushing maiden of the world of washi—soft, delicate, with a gentle sheen and fresh surface. Gampi is like satin and steel, a shimmering surface and brittle strength.

Opposite page, top left: A basket holds a variety of paper things.
Opposite page, photos on right: Mulberry paper has been used for lighting for many hundreds of years and still is one of the best materials for warm light and creative fixtures.

This page, above: *Ikkanbari*, a traditional method of marrying bamboo basketry and paper by pasting on sheets of tough mulberry washi and then reinforcing with persimmon tannin to make the paper waterfast, transforms baskets into containers of surprising strength and unusual beauty. Hisako Hagiwara covers baskets and lanterns with washi and her strong calligraphy, creating sculpted pieces of art .

Left: A papier-mâché shrine maiden by Yoshio Kamata.

Straw

Rice was the grain of the gods. Its byproduct, straw, after earth, was perhaps once Japan's most plentiful material for making things, and the uses to which this ever-available and cheap resource was put startles the imagination. Rice straw was used in clothing, in architecture, for sleeping, for sitting mats, to make footwear of all kinds including sandals and snow boots, for raincoats, hats, baskets and containers, toys

Top: Two bream tied together with straw are a traditional engagement gift. Above: Rice was once the measure of wealth, and the rice bale (*tawara*) was the symbol of prosperity. The art of tying these rice-straw bales, now almost forgotten, is still practiced by a few older men in Niigata and other rice-growing regions. Left: Heavy, rough straw mats, once part of the life of every farm, are now made only as demonstrations at folk life museums and similar places.

and figures, and the great sacred ropes (*shimenawa*) that are used in Shinto shrines. The skills of utilizing this material are quickly dying. Today, mechanized harvesters cut rice stalks too short for making sandals or baskets or the sacred *shimenawa*, and crush the stems as well. In some places, a few special fields are set aside to be harvested by hand to provide rice straw for the craftsmen to use.

**Top: A two-storied stack of straw with roof.
Above: A carefully crafted protective wrapping of straw makes a humble watermelon into a work of art—and also serves as a practical carrying case.
Left: Straw in various forms is still used in gardens to protect and support trees and bushes during the winter.**

This page: Stone has a wide range of uses in the country. Religious carvings, like the folk relief at top and fox figure at left, have a long tradition; the pillars of folk houses rest on stones (above middle); new plastic pipe nests in an old stone drain (above); every region has its own styles of drystone walls (left below).
Opposite: Detail of a path, made by a gardener whose sense of pattern transforms simple river stones into a playful, unexpected design.

Food & Tables

Visits to families in the countryside always amaze me. First of all there is the open-hearted welcome. At festival time, the door is opened wide and the food of the season is offered. Unlike the cities, where food changes with fashion and mood and jigs to the intricacies of the market's distribution system, country food reflects the rhythms of the earth. What is available, what is in season is offered without pretense. The cabbage just picked, the *daikon* radish just pulled from the earth, the bamboo shoot just dug, the fish just caught, each is brought to the table at its finest hour and prepared as simply as possible. In our world of complexity and urban sophistication, it is easy to forget how wonderful simple food is.

SIMMERED KUMQUATS
■ ■ ■ ■ ■ ■ ■ ■ ■ ■ ■ ■ ■ ■ ■ ■

Wash kumquats in lightly salted water, then soak in water for about 1 hour. Drain, then slit deeply 5 times around fruit. Place in saucepan with water to cover and simmer about 1 hour. Drain, cool in basket, and press out seeds. Again cover kumquats with water in saucepan, add generous amount of honey, pinch salt, and some saké or *mirin* (or white wine or sherry) and simmer, half-covered, over low heat for 2 hours. Cool in pan and leave overnight to let flavor mature. Serve 2 or 3 kumquats either chilled or at room temperature. Good as a sweet or as a garnish for meat.

Fire in the House

One-pot cooking around the open irori hearth (opposite) is an inspired feature of winter cuisine. When the dirt-floored kitchen is cold and the irori room is warm, that is where the family will gather and where food will be prepared, with the exception, perhaps, of rice.

Today there are many one-pot recipes, but a one-pot meal for a farming family usually meant just that: whatever was at hand went into the stewpot, usually vegetables and seafood, or vegetables and a little meat, or vegetables and vegetables, sometimes flavored with *miso*, sometimes with soy sauce or, as in the recipe here, with milk. When prosperity increased, then there was time and energy to think of preparing variations and to find out about and enjoy regional differences in one-pot cooking. And there are a surprising number of variations, enough so that there are cookbooks published on the subject, in English as well as Japanese.

Left: Lunch in the country is a coming together of dishes, textiles, and food. The center photo is of a country rice dish simmered with a vegetable (*mukago*) that looks, and tastes somewhat, like tiny potatoes. Opposite page: A country irori set for a warming dinner.

ASUKA NABE
■ ■ ■ ■ ■ ■ ■ ■ ■

3–4 cups fresh chicken stock ◆ 600 gm (1½ lbs) boned chicken, mostly dark meat ◆ 8 *shiitake* mushrooms, cleaned and stemmed ◆ 1 small head Chinese cabbage, steamed, ◆ 200 gm (½ lb) spinach, stemmed, steamed, rinsed quickly, then squeezed of moisture ◆ 3 cups milk ◆ 2 tsps salt ◆ 1 tbsp light soy sauce ◆ ½ tsp sugar ◆ 1 carrot, cut into wedges, parboiled ◆ 450 gm (1 lb) *shirataki* (devil's tongue) noodles, cut into short lengths, parboiled

Place spinach leaves on cabbage leaf pieces, roll and then cut into short tubes. Pour stock into an earthenware *nabe* casserole (or any lidded casserole that can be used over direct heat), add chicken, cabbage-spinach rolls, and shiitake mushrooms. Cover and cook 3–4 minutes. Remove any foam. Add milk, salt, soy sauce, and sugar, carrot, and shirataki noodles. Cook 5–6 minutes over medium heat. It is ready. This is best cooked on a tabletop cooking unit, but it can be cooked in the kitchen and brought to the table. Let everyone help themselves to this warming dish and its broth, a specialty of the ancient Asuka region near Nara.

There are no limits and no restraints on what can be done with things from the country, both old and new. Here a section of split green bamboo stalk lined with a leaf from the garden is good for serving cookies. Tea served in cups by pottter Masanao Kusumoto is arranged on an old indigo-striped hemp textile. Who would believe that this fabric, once used as horse reins and long forgotten, would wind up as an attractive table cloth and be appreciated for its own sake.

SESAME COOKIES
■ ■ ■ ■ ■ ■ ■ ■ ■ ■ ■ ■

³/₄ cup butter ◆ ¹/₂ cup brown sugar ◆ ¹/₂ cup white sugar
◆ 1 egg ◆ 1¹/₄ cups sifted flour ◆ 1 tsp salt ◆ ³/₄ cup
roasted sesame seeds

Mix together butter, sugars, and egg. Mix in remaining
ingredients.

Place rounded teaspoonfulls on buttered cookie sheet. Bake
4–5 minutes at 180°C (350°F). Makes 4¹/₂ dozen cookies.

Food and Vessels

One without the other is incomplete and un-fulfilled. Country cooking, the honest taste of what is in season, fresh from the garden, river, and sea, invites dishes and vessels that complement the food. Nothing flashy or gaudy, but things handmade by potter or woodworker or lacquerer, glass-blower or basket maker — things whose color, shape, and texture enhance and make more delicious the food that is served. In Japan, every food is served to a diner in its own dish; this involves an aesthetic very different from using one plate to hold quantities of different foods. The art of food arrangement (*moritsuke*) reached the heights it did in Japan probably because there were so many kinds of vessels made of many different materials. Let your instinct, not the head, tell you what vessel to use with which food. The only principle is not to fill the vessel so full that it is no longer visible. Less is more. And at the right time and place, serve food on fresh leaves, on a slab of wood, or on flat stones.

Lunch in the Hagiwara house is fascinating—beans in yellow rice, a vegetable stew, vegetables dressed with grated apple and daikon radish—inspired vegetarian fare made at the moment from what is at hand. Vessels, food, the house, the ambience, Hisako Hagiwara herself, each and all have a strength of character that form a cohesive, enchanting whole.

Above; An old lacquer tub
becomes a refrigerator for
vegetables stored in a cool place
in front of a storeroom door.
Left: Each pot and dish in the
Uchida kitchen, however
ordinary, has a certain beauty.

Photos left and below: The cheerful, stylish tables of Miwako Kimura and her family burst with colorful, festive food prepared for friends and family invited to celebrate the Japanese New Year. Everyone participates, everyone enters into the spirit of new beginnings. Old-fashioned games prepared by the children are enjoyed by all. Festivities and food are interconnected, and food, not to mention drink, is the highlight of the celebration. With this in mind, Kimura-san has paid special attention to creating food arrangements that impress the eye with a sense of high-spirited fun.

Top left: Hand-gathered wild mushrooms dry on simple basket trays.

Top right: These tasty-looking dumplings are country cockroach control, a natural recipe to rid a house of these pests.

Right: Fish grill on skewers while the pot simmers over an *irori*.

Below: At the Sakamoto inn on the Noto Peninsula, a charcoal fire is used to grill slices of daikon radish and freshly caught sardines and crab. The buckwheat (*soba*) noodles, a specialty of the house, are made from local buckwheat and are reason enough by themselves to make the effort to come here.

A fine old door from a traditional country storehouse (*kura*) makes a spectacular table. Here the vintage samurai banner under glass completes the table arrangement. Trays frame an elegant lunch as delicious as it is beautiful.

Flavored rice balls (*onigiri*) complement a country casserole of pumpkin and pork slices stewed in a miso sauce. Large autumn leaves serve as plates that can be thrown away without remorse.

New country tastes: A variety of dishes and vessels and textiles are brought together in an innovative way to meet the mood of the day. The lunch is of mini rice balls of all shapes and sizes, gingered eggplant, a warm

tofu salad, and salads of cucumber with *shiso* (beef steak plant) leaves and julienned daikon radish with scallops, all on a sunny blue-and-white tablecloth. On another tray, a meal in a bowl features pork cutlet in soy and egg on a bowl of rice.

158

GINGERED EGGPLANT
■ ■ ■ ■ ■ ■ ■ ■ ■ ■ ■ ■ ■ ■ ■

1½ Tbsps soy sauce ◆ 1 tsp saké ◆ 1 tsp vinegar ◆ thumb-sized knob of fresh ginger, peeled and finely grated ◆ 6 small eggplants ◆ vegetable oil for deep-frying

Make ginger sauce by mixing soy sauce, saké, vinegar, and grated ginger in a bowl.

Heat oil to medium hot. Cut eggplants in half and score skin side in a crosshatch pattern. Pat dry and deep-fry until cut side is light gold. Immerse in sauce while still hot. May be eaten hot or cold.

THE COLOR OF THE LAND

Once in an antique shop, I encountered a sample book in which some-one—a dyer probably—had pasted swatches of solid indigo-dyed cotton. It must have had twenty or thirty pages with perhaps ten different shades of indigo on each page. Think of it! Three hundred shades of blue! Each had a special name and special directions for how many times the cloth should be dipped into the dye, as well as dye recipes. I still feel as many shades of regret for not having bought that book.

On reflection, however, three hundred subtle shades of indigo blue is not so surprising in Japan, because the land itself is indigo, and nature in the countryside joyfully displays countless variations and permutations of blue daily. Whatever it is that is responsible for this phenomenon—light, humidity, dust, weather—Japan is truly a land of indigo, from the soft washes of the sky to the assertive, deep blues of the mountains to the gray-blues of the surrounding seas. And indigo, naturally, became the color of the clothing and textiles of the people who inhabited this countryside.

Indigo was part of every aspect of country life. Visitors to Japan at the end of the nineteenth century often remarked on the countryside of blue. It was the color of work, and Japan was a country of workers and craftsmen—the farmer bent over his field, the carpenter astride his lumber, the fisherman pulling in nets, the potter kneading clay—all wore indigo clothes.

The household loom was part of country life. Though a country weaver might attain great skill, with a life of constant labor and poverty, fancy textiles and fancy dyes that faded were unthinkable. Indigo leaves were grown on the farm, then taken to the village to be used by the dyer for that area. Indigo is a vat dye and needs no mordant. A dip into the vat is all that is necessary—the longer the exposure to the dye, the deeper the blue. It was the ideal dye for a hard life, and is one of mankind's most

ancient and most widely used dyes for this good reason.

Developed from methods and materials borrowed from Asian antecedents, Japan's textile tradition developed techniques of weaving and dyeing unique in their sensitivity of design and refinement of skill. Country dyers managed to create a bright, fresh rainbow of shades and tones with just two basic colors: blue and white. What an amazing variety of expression they captured and preserved in the magical realm of indigo.

Cotton became the fabric of the countryside during the last century. Before cotton, textiles of bast fibers like hemp and ramie and the fibers of wild vines were common in the countryside, but such fabrics do not keep you warm, and the fibers, although very strong, are uncomfortable and scratchy. All types of clothing, banners, working gear, and household textiles were dyed in shades of blue. When indigo was combined with other colors, such companion shades were always earth tones—browns, umbers, saffron reds, yellows, and rusts. Indigo was king, and all its com-

panions blended and matched. The symphony of quiet natural colors of those days still amazes when we see and touch the old textiles.

Indigo was not only for wearing. Blue-and-white (*furoshiki*) carrying cloths

were for bundles large and small. Futon bedding quilts were covered in plain blue or blue-and-white designs. Mosquito netting, traditionally woven of hemp, was carefully sewn into huge, bottomless cubes, which were hung from the rafters to fill a room. These were dyed in graduated shades of blue or in green, which was obtained by overdyeing indigo with the yellow of gardenia pods. The reputed efficacy of indigo as an insect and snake repellant made it ideal for mosquito netting and farm clothes.

Throughout the land, country people delighted in the endless variety of design and color that the marriage of cotton and indigo produced, ingenious results of the dyeing art of Japan, one of the many wonders in the cultural treasure chest of Japanese textiles.

Shown opposite and top is the workshop of Hiroyuki Shindo, an indigo dyer and a highly respected artist in Japan. It took Shindo six months to dig the pit in which to sink the large stoneware indigo vats. Only the vat mouths now poke up above the dirt floor of the old doma work area of the house, concealing the huge pots of living, fermenting indigo, which foams beneath the surface and embues Shindo's specially woven hemp and ramie materials with the most magical blue to be found anywhere. ◪

Hisako Hagiwara has developed her own distinctive style of sashiko. Reminiscent of primitive African textiles, her sashiko pieces are textural works that do not need to be seen to be appreciated—their knobs and bumps can be felt. She herself wears the beautiful hemp and banana fiber kimonos that she finds in antique shops and then mends with strong, expressive stitches of thick cotton threads, adding color and design to what she has found. Her style of dress, like her style of sashiko, creates surprise and elicits questions wherever she goes.

Sashiko

Sashiko is a basic quilting stitch, traditionally unbleached hemp thread sewn on an indigo ground, to reinforce layers of work clothes for warmth and strength, although sometimes only a single cloth is stitched, as with furoshiki. In the Tohoku region of the north, young girls would show their flare for needlework in elaborate jackets stitched for their trousseaus. The painstaking sashiko that came out of those dark northern winters is testimony to the patience and endurance of country women.

Above: Patchwork futon cover made of sashiko and hand towels. This is the work of a country woman who valued the hand towels she was given over the years and pieced them together with sashiko stitchery—evidence of the patience as well as the timeless sense of design of the country grandmother.
Right: A sashiko fisherman's jacket from Wakasa Bay, a distinctive design that alternates squares of *kasuri* (see page 172) with the geometric hemp flower pattern in sashiko stichery.
Below: A contemporary kimono by Kazuko Yoshimura, who has sewn a sampler of sashiko patterns with the segments of a cracked ice design.

Shibori

Shibori is a large family of resist dyeing techniques that have in common shaping the fabric before dyeing, then returning the cloth to its two-dimensional form afterwards. Tie-dyeing is but one type of shibori, and among the other techniques are stitching, capping, binding, core-wrapping, pole-wrapping, clamping with boards (both plain and carved), tub-stuffing, and many many others. The effects that can be achieved with shibori seem endless, but they all rely on random events that happen when dye is absorbed into fabric that has been shaped and that shape held firmly by various means to create a resist. The interaction of indigo and cotton, particularly, produces wonderful nuances of color tone when combined with shibori.

Opposite: Traditional Japanese diapers are now collector's items. They were dyed in blue using board-clamping and other types of shibori.

Left: A checkerboard textile of indigo-dyed hemp by Hiroyuki Shindo moves gently in the breeze on the veranda of his thatched house.

Below: The bold design of this piece of shibori-dyed hemp by Seizo Ishikawa, a farmer, seems at home working as a scarecrow by a newly harvested rice field.

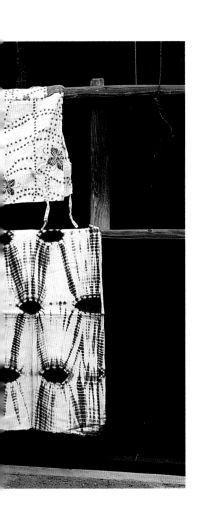

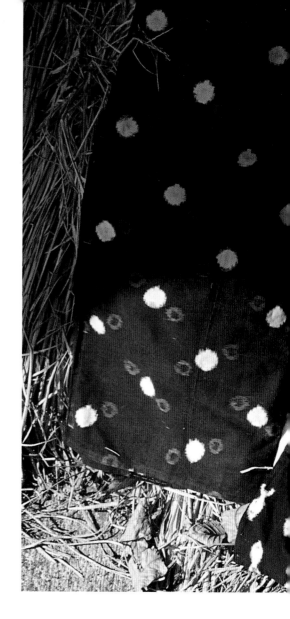

Kasuri (Ikat)

Resist-binding threads in calculated patterns or designs before dyeing then weaving these threads after dyeing produces an effect of designs or motifs with soft, blurry edges. The most famous examples of this effect are the brightly colored Indonesian ikats, and in Japan the same technique is used to produce the more sober but no less delightful *kasuri* fabrics. Kasuri is particularly associated with women's indigo work clothes, with indigo quilt covers, and with men's kimono. The range of pattern is great, varying from minute, abstract motifs to bold geometric and pictorial designs.

Opposite: Perfectly simple, a child's checked kasuri kimono. Left: A kasuri bedspread animates a bedroom-*cum*-study. Above: Kasuri samplers: bits and bobs of kasuri pieces have humor and surprise.

173

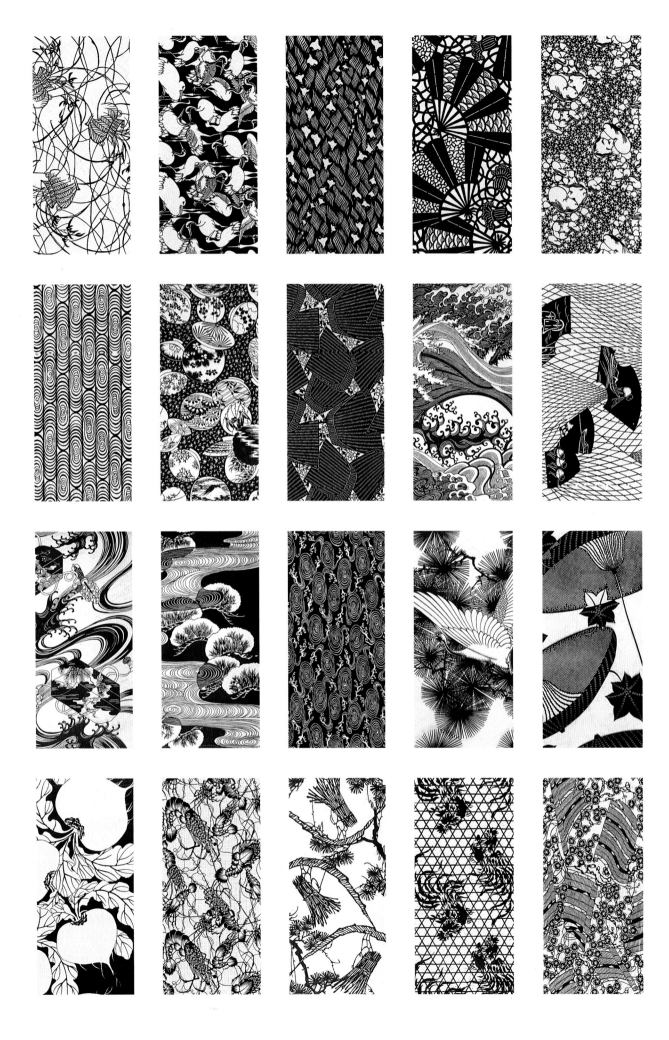

Opposite: Stencils of every kind.
Left: This padded sleeping kimono (*yogi*) of striped indigo hemp shows a vigorous yet simple sense of design.
Below: An unusual kimono with a wonderful design of a turnip on an indigo background.
Bottom: A heavy indigo yogi airs on a pole outside the Miyatani house, in the countryside near Wajima in western Japan.

Stencil Dyeing

Japanese stencils for stencil dyeing are an art form in themselves. Layers of handmade mulberry paper are reinforced and waterproofed with persimmon tannin, then cut by master craftsmen into delicate and inventive stencils whose designs are based on the natural world. A stencil is placed on the fabric, paste resist is applied with a spatula, and the stencil removed. The fabric is dyed when the paste resist is set, then the paste is washed away after dyeing is completed. Stencil resist of this kind results in designs of great refinement and beauty.

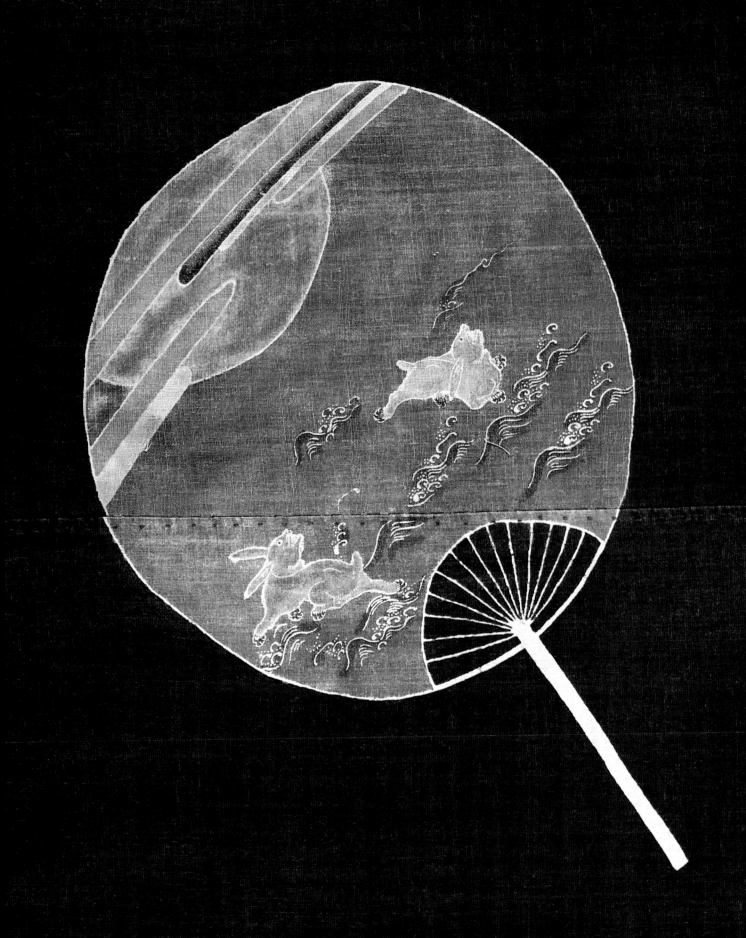

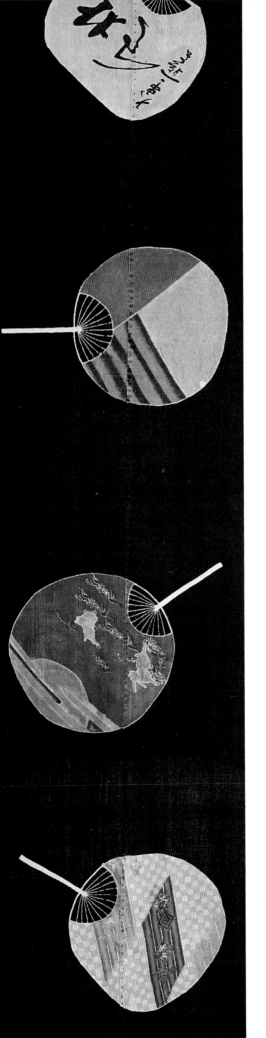

Tsutsugaki

The *tsutsugaki* technique involves freely drawn designs using paste resist applied to the textile surface with a paper cone, like a cake decorator. The whole textile is dipped in indigo, and other colors are applied by brush later. The country dyer made tsutsugaki fabrics for such uses as bedding, wrapping cloths, and banners with a freehand style and whimsical directness that still capture our hearts and make tsutsugaki among the most sought after of country textiles. The freshness of approach and spontaneity of design hardly reveal that these were usually traditional auspicious designs used as celebratory textiles for weddings, births, and to celebrate longevity.

Left: Monkeys were gods of the barn, divine protectors of horses, and therefore a popular motif for horse trappings.
Below: A humorous crane tries to keep its feet out of the waves cresting on the bottom of a celebratory jacket, perhaps for a man's sixtieth birthday.

Opposite left: A long, narrow nineteenth century tsutsugaki textile of beautiful, intricate designs within fan shapes was probably a stage curtain.
Opposite right: The roundels of graceful designs from nature in this sleeping kimono show some of the delicacy possible with tsutsugaki dyeing.
Opposite bottom: A playful design of a rabbit leaping over waves on a horse trapping from the north of Japan.

Opposite: A rare signed tsutsugaki futon cover with a design of nightingales and plum tree and an elaborate family crest, framed and backed in blue-and-white stripes and filled with heavy batting for warm sleep. Above right: Peaches, baskets, and family crest on an early and much-mended furoshiki. Above left: Wrapping became art with a furoshiki like this displaying an arabesque background and stylized characters. Left: Rabbits cavort among waves in a horse trapping with an unusual crest. Bottom left: A faithful old couple with cranes, turtles, plum, bamboo, and pine—a grand outpouring of auspicious symbols—fill this baby's bath cloth from Izumo. Bottom right: Two fierce *baku*, mythological animals that eat bad dreams, are an appropriate theme for sleeping futon.

Left: Carp climbing a waterfall are symbols of male courage and determination—a popular theme in country textiles, as in this sleeping kimono.
Below: New Year's shrine jacket with a sacred rope shimenawa and rising sun.

Below: Stylized gray clouds and red lightning bolts cover the entire surface of this intriguing cotton garment.
Right: A bright shrimp design on an old horse textile invokes long life and prosperity.

Opposite page: Carp climbing waterfalls were symbols of masculine bravery and strength, and were often used in yogi sleeping kimono.

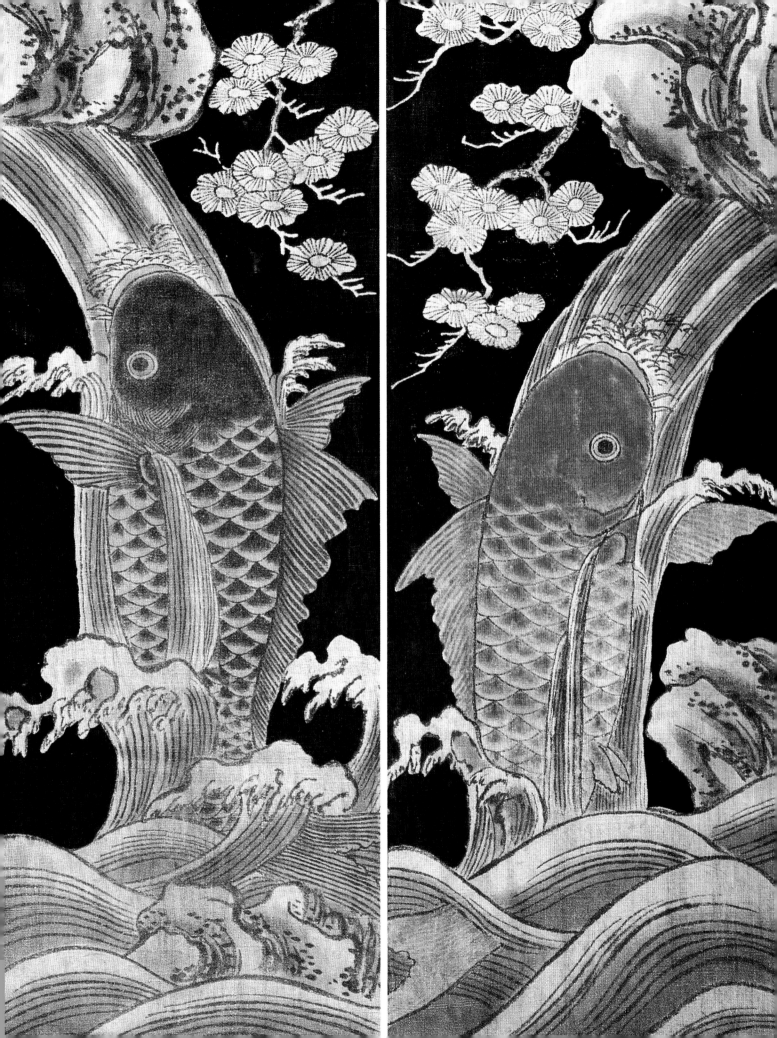

Left: Cushions covered with ragweave and (below) a rag-weave rug, both in restored farmhouses. Bottom: Rag ropes for hauling, carrying, hanging, and decorating. Right: Vests for work and (below) all the makings for rag weaving and making slippers. Opposite: A ragweave vest, probably from Sado Island, Is at least fifty years old but perfectly wearable today.

Rags and Patches

Recycling was a way of life in country Japan. Worn-out clothing would be used to patch bedding, and old bedding was cut into squares, which were stitched together to make dust cloths. At the end of the cycle, old fabrics were torn into strips, twisted, and woven into cloth. In the countryside, ragweave was used for work garments for both farmer and fisherman as well as for quilt covers, kotatsu covers, and even floor coverings.

Until only recently, Japan was a nation of inveterate menders. Particularly in the country, mending became a fine art. Japanese quilting (sashiko) was itself originally a form of mending and reinforcing for warmth. The patterns and motifs of the stitchery are true celebrations—practicality transformed into pleasure. When digging through piles of old textiles at flea markets, one often encounters mends—always on the inside. Each mend reveals the heart of the mender—the deftness and delicacy of a grandmother, the resolute yet self-effacing stitches of a young wife, the awkward and earnest efforts of a young girl. Their stories are there in the stitches.

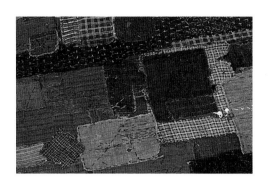

Sometimes one encounters generations of patches on a single garment—patches upon patches upon patches—and such pieces may be beautiful works of art in themselves and for what they reveal of toil and endurance.

The overall effect of the combination of stitching and patching to extend the life of a garment or textile gives a feeling of persistence, of resourcefulness and a stubborn refusal to give up. When I see these patches and mends, brave testimonials to times of biting hardship, I rejoice first of all in their tenderness and beauty, and then I catch my breath and think of the true meaning of what they say—the direness of the times, the preciousness of things, and I am moved.

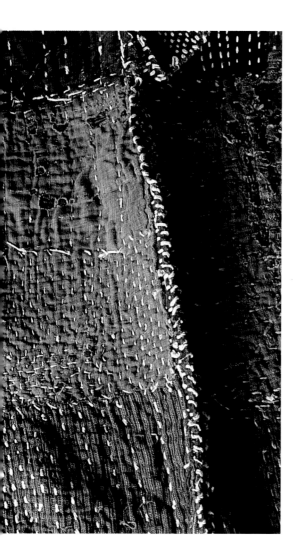

Opposite top: An old loom for weaving straw mats, its wood gleaming from long use, makes a fine stand for displaying a patched bedcover.
Left: A fisherman's coat, thick with layer upon layer of patches, is reinforced by *sashiko* stitchery.
Above: Patched futon on beds and a ragweave rug in a restored farmhouse.

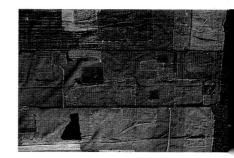

Ragweave and patched and mended work clothes. The miraculous thing is that so many such pieces are extant today, carefully stored away for decades by the families that made and used them.

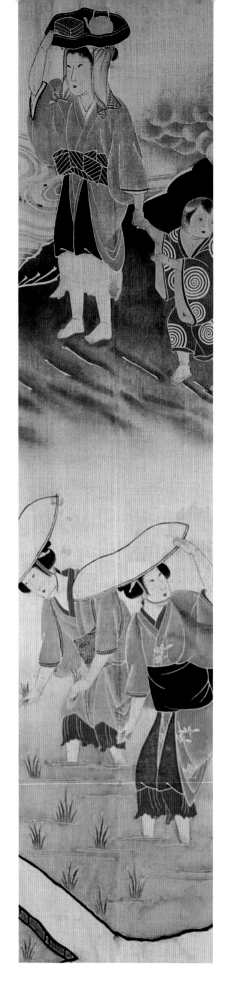

SOURCES

In Tokyo and Yokohama

SHOPS ◆ *Beniya* (folk crafts) 4-20-19 Minami Aoyama, Minato-ku, Tokyo. Tel: (03) 3403-8115. ◆ *Bingoya* (folk crafts, toys) 10-6 Wakamatsu-cho, Shinjuku, Tokyo. Tel: (03) 3202-8778. ◆ *Folk Craft Ebine* (folk crafts) New Gaien Heights, 4-5-1 Sendagaya, Shibuya-ku, Tokyo. Tel. (03) 3408-9380 ◆ *Savoir Vivre* (contemporary ceramics) AXIS Bldg. 3F., 5-17-1 Roppongi, Minato-ku, Tokyo. Tel: (03) 3585-7365. ◆ *Sei* (indigo textiles) Hanae Mori Bldg., basement, 3-6-1 Kita Aoyama, Minato-ku, Tokyo. Tel: (03) 3407-7541. ◆ *Takumi* (folk crafts) 8-4-2 Ginza, Chuo-ku, Tokyo. Tel: (03) 3571-2017. ◆ *Toukyo* (contemporary ceramics) 2-25-13 Nishi Azabu, Minato-ku, Tokyo. Tel: (03) 3797-4494.

ANTIQUE SHOPS ◆ *Akariya*, 4-8-1 Yoyogi, Shibuya-ku, Tokyo. Tel: (03) 3465-5578. ◆ *Antique Gallery Meguro*, Stork Mansion, 201, 2-24-18 Kami Osaki, Shinagawa-ku, Tokyo. Tel: (03) 3493-1971. ◆ *Bo Peep*, 1230 Naganuma cho, Hachioji-shi, Tokyo. Tel. 0426-35-1540. ◆ *Gallery Kawano* (vintage textiles) 4-4-9 Jingumae, Shibuya-ku, Tokyo. Tel: (03) 3470-3305. ◆ *Hobo*, 2-8-2 Azabu Juban, Minato-ku, Tokyo. Tel/Fax: (03) 5442-9432. ◆ *Kurofune*, 7-7-4 Roppongi, Minato-ku, Tokyo. Tel: (03) 3479-1552. ◆ *Makotoya*, 2-39-2 Wada, Suginami-ku, Tokyo. Tel: (03) 3311-1609. ◆ *Morita Antiques*, 5-12-2 Minami Aoyama, Minato-ku, Tokyo. Tel: (03) 3407-4466. ◆ *Okura Oriental Art*, 3-3-14 Azabudai, Minato-ku, Tokyo. Tel: (03) 3585-5309. ◆ *Omoshiroya*, 1-11-21-101 Kichijo-ji Higashi-cho, Musashino-shi, Tokyo. Tel: 0422-22-8565. ◆ *Saruyama*, 3-12-46- #101 Moto Azabu, Minato-ku, Tokyo. Tel: (090) 4536-0196. ◆ *Tamiser*, 2-11-6- #201 Moto Azabu, Minato-ku, Tokyo. Tel: (03) 5443-9066. ◆ *Uchida* (earthy pottery, textiles, lacquer, glass) 2-8-6 Azabu Juban, Minato-ku, Tokyo. Tel: (03) 3455-4595.

MUSEUMS ◆ *Japan Folkcraft Museum* (Nihon Mingeikan), 4-3-33 Komaba, Meguro-ku, Tokyo. Tel: (03) 3467-4527.

In the Country

COUNTRY ANTIQUES ◆ *Gallery Kawano* (vintage textiles) 15 Okinohata, Yanagawa, Fukuoka Prefecture. Tel: 0944-73-0131. ◆ *Gallery Mu*, Muudani, Oizumi Mura, Kita Komagun, Yamanashi Prefecture. Tel: 0551-38-0061. ◆ *Gozaku*, 1-31 Konyacho, Morioka-shi, Iwate-ken. Tel: 019-622-7129. ◆ *Gungendo Iwamiginzan Honten*, Ha 183, Omoricho, Otashi, Shimane-ken 694-0305. Tel: 0854-89-0077. ◆ *Gungendo Kyoto-ten*, 6-11 Obayashicho, Shugakuin, Sakyo-ku, Kyoto-shi, Kyoto-fu 606-8081. Tel: 075-705-3515. ◆ *House of Antiques*, Yoshihiro Takishita, 5-15-5 Kajiwara, Kamakura-shi, Kanagawa Prefecture. Fax: 0467-43-7338. ◆ *Kakitani Antiques*, 212-6 Kita-Akitsu, Tokorozawa-shi, Saitama Prefecture. Tel: 0429-95-0626. ◆ *Kamasada Cast Ironworks (Nobuho Miya)* 2-5 Konyacho, Moriokashi, Iwate-ken. Tel: 019-622 3912. ◆ *Kochinoya*, Imaeda Sanae, Toba 80, Takaya-cho, Konan-shi, Aichi Prefecture. Tel: 0587-55-3314. ◆ *Kurahachi*, 5 Shimoni no Machi, Takayama shi, Gifu Prefecture. Tel: 0577-32-3600.

SHOPS ◆ *Blue & White*, 2-9-2 Azabu Juban, Minato-ku, Tokyo 106-0045. Tel: (03) 3451-0537. ◆ *Bura House*, Ha-185 Oomori-cho, Ota-shi, Shimane-ken. Tel: 08548-9-0131. ◆ *Gungendo*, Kyoto, 6-11 Dourin-cho, Shugaku-in, Sakyo-ku, Kyoto-shi, Kyoto. Tel/Fax: 075-705-3515. ◆ *Hyugaji*, 1-16-5 Hiroshima, Miyazaki-shi, Miyazaki Prefecture. Tel: 0985-22-8338. ◆ *Kame no Ii Craft Shop*, see Kame no Ii (Inns). ◆ *Kogensha*, 2 Zaimokucho, Morioka-shi, Iwate Prefecture. Tel: 019-622-2894. ◆ *Kosoen Indigo Dyers*, 8-200 Nagabuchi, Ome Shi, Tokyo. Tel: 0428-24-8121 ◆ *Moyai Kogei*, 2-1-10 Sasuke, Kamakura, Kanagawa Prefecture. Tel: 0467-22-1822. ◆ *Tefu Tefu*, Asa Ichi Dori 3-chome, Kawai-machi, Wajima-shi, Ishikawa Prefecture. Tel: 0768-22-6304. ◆ *Yu Craft*, 10-7 Saiwai-cho, Kanazawa-shi, Ishikawa Prefecture. Tel/Fax: 0762-24-0015.

INNS ◆ *Kame no Ii Besso*, 2633-1 Kawakami, Yufuin-cho, Oita-gun, Oita Prefecture. Tel: 0977-84-3166. ◆ *Kurashiki Ryokan*, 4-1 Honmachi, Kurashiki-shi, Okayama Prefecture. Tel: 0864-22-0730. ◆ *Miyamaso*, Harachi-cho 375, Hanase, Sakyo-ku, Kyoto. Tel: 0757-46-0231. ◆ *Sakamoto Ryokan*, Jisha, Uedo-machi, Suzushi, Ishikawa Prefecture. Tel: 0768-82-0584. ◆ *Sanso Murata*, 1264-2 Torigoe, Kawakami, Yufinmachi, Oita-gun, Oita Prefecture. Tel: 0977-84-5000. ◆ *Tamano yo*, Yunotsubo, Yufuin Onsen, Oita Prefecture. Tel: 0977-84-2158. ◆ *Yoyokaku*, 2-4-40 Higashi Karatsu Karatsu-shi, Saga Prefecture. Tel: 0955-72-7181.

MUSEUMS ◆ *Chido Museum*, Chido Hakubutsukan, 10-18 Kachushinmachi, Tsuruoka, Yamagata Prefecture. Tel: 0235-22-1604. ◆ *Gunma Prefectural Museum of History*, 239 Iwahana-cho, Takasaki-shi, Gunma Prefecture 370-12. Tel: 0273-46-5522. ◆ *Hakusan Roku Minzoku Shiryokan*, Hakusan Folk Museum, Azashiramine Ri-30, Shiramine Mura, Ishikawa-gun, Ishikawa Prefecture. Tel: 0761-98-2665. ◆ *Izumo Folk Craft Museum* (Mingeikan), 628 Chiimiya-cho, Izumo-shi, Shimane Prefecture. Tel: 0853-22-6397. ◆ *Kurashiki Museum*, 1-4-11 Chuo, Kurashiki-shi, Okayama Prefecture. Tel: 0864-22-1637. ◆ *Kusano Family Residence*, Kusano Honke, 11-4 Mamedamachi, Hita-shi, Oita Prefecture. Tel: 0973-24-4110. ◆ *Matsumoto Folk Craft Museum*, 1313-1 Shimoganai, Satoyamabe, Matsumoto-shi, Nagano Prefecture. Tel: 0263-33-1569. ◆ *Nihon Minkaen* (a collection of folk houses from around the country) 7-1-1 Masukata, Tama-ku, Kawasaki-shi, Kanagawa Prefecture. Tel: 0449-22-2181. ◆ *Shikoku Mura*, 91 Nakamachi, Yashima, Takamatsu-shi, Kagawa Prefecture 761-01. Tel: 0878-43-3111. ◆ *Toyama Kinenkan*, 675 Shiroinuma, Kawajimachi, Hikigun, Saitama Prefecture. Tel: 049-297-0007.

Craftspeople

BAMBOO WORKERS ◆ *Moriya*, Masaharu, Moriya Bamboo, 306 Kurogane-cho, Aoba-ku, Yokohamashi, Kanagawa Prefecture. Tel: 0459-71-2028.

CANDLESTICK MAKERS ◆ *Mishima*, Junji, 3-12 Ichino Machi, Furukawa-cho, Yoshiki-gun, Gifu Prefecture. Tel: 0577-73-4109.

POTTERS ◆ *Nakazato*, Takashi, 4331-1 Mirukashi, Karatsu, Saga Prefecture. Tel: 0955-74-3503. Also sold at Yoyokaku Inn, Karatsu, Saga Prefecture, see above ◆ *Toukyo*, Ishihara Bldg., 2-25-13 Nishi Azabu, Minato-ku, Tokyo. Tel: (03) 3797-4494. ◆ *Uchida*, 2-8-6, Azabu Juban, Minato-ku, Tokyo.

PAPERMAKERS ◆ *Awagami Factory*, URL/http://www.awagami.or.jp Tel: 0883-42-6120. ◆ *Idani Shinji* (e-mail Hiikawa@bs.kkm.ne.jp), 302 Kamikumatani, Mitoya-cho, Iishi-gun, Shimane Prefecture. Tel: 690-2511. ◆ *Keijusha*, 668 Kagami-machi, Yatsuo-machi, Nei-gun, Toyama Prefecture. Tel: 939-2341. ◆ *Noto Nigyo Washi*, Mii-machi, Wajima-shi Ishikawa Prefecture. Tel: 0768-26-1314. ◆ *Paper Nao*, 4-37-28 Hakusan bunkyo-ku, Tokyo. Tel: (03) 3944-4470.

STRAW CRAFTSMEN ◆ *Yanagida*, Toshinaka, available at Blue & White, 2-9-2 Azabu Juban, Minato-ku, Tokyo. Tel: (03) 3451-0537.

THATCHERS ◆ *Makoto*, Nakano, Kitamura Kayabuki Yane Koji, Kitamura Thatched Roof Construction, 13 Kita Miyama Kitakuwada, Kyoto. Tel/Fax: 0771-77-0649. ◆ *Shimomura*, Nabuyoshi (also does restoring), 8 Asahi Shinasahi-cho, Takashima-gun, Shiga Prefecture. Tel: 0740-25-4370. ◆ *Yamazaki*, Tatsunosuke, Shizuhara, Miyama-cho, Kitakawada-gun, Kyoto-fu. Tel: 0771-75-0574.

LANDSCAPE GARDENER ◆ *Marc Peter Keane*, Landscape Architect. Kotobuki Bldg., 5F, Kawaramachi Shijo Sagaru, Shimogyoku, Kyoto-fu 600. Tel/Fax: 075-352-5353.

WOODWORKERS ◆ *Woodruff*, Douglas, 19 Azatorii, Keihoku-cho, Kitakuwata-gun, Kyoto-fu, 601-03. Tel: 0771-53-0751; Fax: 0771-53-0661.

Books

◆ Bess, Nancy Moore. *Bamboo in Japan*. Kodonsha International, 2001. ◆ Brandon, Reiko Mochinaga. *Country Textiles of Japan*. New York, Tokyo: Weatherhill, 1986. ◆ Hauge, Victor and Takako. *Folk Traditions in Japanese Art*. New York, Tokyo: Weatherhill, 1973. ◆ Hibi, Sadao, ed. *Japanese Tradition in Color and Form*. Tokyo: Graphic-sha Publication Co., Ltd., 1987. ◆ Hotta, Ann, with Ishiguro, Yoko. *A Guide to Japanese Hotsprings*. Tokyo, New York, San Francisco: Kodansha International, 1986. ◆ Inagaki, Takamasa. *Views of a Japanese Village*. Tokyo: Graphic-sha Publication Co., Ltd., 1992. ◆ Japan Folk Crafts Museum. *Mingei: Masterpieces of Japanese Folkcraft*. Tokyo, New York, San Francisco: Kodansha International Ltd., 1991. ◆ Katoh, Amy Sylvester. *Japan: The Art of Living*. Tokyo and Rutland, Vermont: Charles E. Tuttle Company, 1990. ◆ Kawashima, Chuji. *Minka: Traditional Houses of Rural Japan*. Tokyo, New York, San Francisco: Kodansha International Ltd., 1986. ◆ Kinoshita, June and Palevsky, Nicholas. *Gateway to Japan*. Tokyo, New York, San Francisco: Kodansha International, 1990. ◆ Manning, Theodore. *Flea Markets of Japan, A Pocket Guide for Antique Buyers*. Tokyo, New York, London: Kodansha International, 2003. Massy, Patricia. *Sketches of Japanese Crafts*. Tokyo: Japan Times, 1980. ◆ Morse, Edward, Sylvester. *Japanese Homes and Their Surroundings*. Tokyo and Rutland, Vermont: Charles E. Tuttle Company, 1972. ◆ Saga, Dr. Junichi. *Memories of Straw and Silk*. Tokyo, New York, San Francisco: Kodansha International Ltd., 1990. ◆ Sekijima, Hisako. *Basketry*. Tokyo, New York, San Francisco: Kodansha International Ltd., 1986. ◆ Shimojima, Masao. *The Art of Matchbox Labels*. Tokyo: Shinshindo Shuppan Co., Ltd., 1989. ◆ Tanaka, Ikko, et. al. *Japan Design*. Tokyo: Libro Port Company, Ltd., 1984. ◆ Tanaka, Ikko, et. al. *Japanese Coloring*. Tokyo: Libro Port Company, Ltd., 1984. ◆ Tanizaki, Junichiro. *In Praise of Shadows*. Tokyo and Rutland, Vermont: Charles E. Tuttle Company, 1984. ◆ Ueda, Atsushi. *Inner Harmony of the Japanese House*. Tokyo, New York, San Francisco: Kodansha International, 1990. ◆ Yanagi Soetsu, *Folk Crafts in Japan*. Tokyo: Kokusai Bunka Shinkokai, 1949. ◆ Yoshida, Mitsukuni, et. al. *Japanese Style*. Tokyo, New York, San Francisco: Kodansha International Ltd., 1980. ◆ Uemura, Masaharo, *Rediscovering Old Japan*. Yohan Shuppan KK, Tokyo, 2000, 2003.

Flea Markets

◆ First Saturday of the Month: *Azabu Juban Patio*, Azabu Juben Station. Exit 4 on the Nambollo Line or Oedo Line. ◆ First Sunday of the Month: *Arai Yakushi Temple*, Arai Yakushijimae Station on the Seibu Shinjuku Line. ◆ First and fourth Sundays: *Togo Shrine*, Harajuku Station on the Yamanote Line or Meiji Jingumae Station on the Chiyoda Line. ◆ Second Sunday: *Kumagawa Jinja*, Fussa Shi, Nogi Shrine, Nogizaka Station on the Chiyoda Line. ◆ Second and third Sundays: *Hanazono Shrine*, Shinjuku-san-chome Station on the Marunouchi Line. ◆ Fourth Sunday of the Month: *Suwa Shrine*, Tachikawa, 1-5-15, Shibasaki-cho, Tachikawa –shi, Tokyo, Tel: 042-522-2968. ◆ Every Sunday of the Month: *Hanazono Shrine*, Shinjuku-san-chome Station on the Marunochi Line ◆ Fourth Thursday and Friday: *Roi Building*, Roppongi Station on the Hibiya Line. ◆ 21st of the Month: *Toji Shrine*, Kyoto. ◆ 25th of the Month: *Kitano Shrine*, Kyoto. ◆ 28th of the Month: *Narita Fudo Shrine*, Kawagome, Saitama Prefecture on the Tobu Tojo Line. ◆ December 15, 16 and January 15, 16: *Boro Ichi*, Setagaya Station on the Setagaya Line (private). ◆ March, June, September, December: *Heiwajima Antiques Fair*, Ryutsu Center Station on the Tokyo Monorail from Hamamatsucho Station on the Yamanote Line.

Shunju Restaurant, Tokyo.

Where does Japan's country road lead to from here, now that the country scene seems bleak? Restoring old folk houses is for the rich and dedicated. Unthinking destruction has always been much easier than expensive preservation. Many people cannot work out how to fit those quaint old country houses into their fast-paced lives. It is easier to just tear them down and start afresh.

But tradition is never totally destroyed. Nature and the seasons call out to us even in our concrete environment. The wisdom and beauty of the country remain compelling, coaxing some city dwellers to incorporate this spirit into their urban lives.

One such person is Harumi Nibe. There is no convenient label for Nibe-san. She arranges flowers and makes food, but like no one else. She breaks all the rules. She uses flowers picked from the roadside or from her own garden—nothing else. She arranges them in whatever inspires, whether it is a pile of pot shards, an open drawer, even empty unused bottles. In this she is, perhaps unwittingly, picking up the spirit of country Japan, with its history of not only making do with what is available, but making what is available beautiful—the future of country Japan? ■